# NUMEROLOGY:

## *Life's Mirror of Vibration*

by

*John Lawrence Maerz*

# *books by* John Lawrence Maerz

- **TAROT**: *The Astrological Layout*
- **CYCLES**: *The Application of Energy Within the Natural Cycle*
- **IS ANYONE THERE?** *Reaching Across the Veil in Mediumship*
- **ENERGIZING SELF-TRUST**: *7 Steps for Reclaiming Your Power*
- **OUT OF THE BOX**: *7 Elements for Raising a Self-Directing Child*
- **SIGNS & PORTENTS**: *A Reader's Guide for Combining Psychic Tools*
- **PLOYS FOR DOMINANCE**: *A Guide for Recognizing & Disarming Manipulation*
- **NUMEROLOGY**: *Life's Mirror of Vibration*
- **ASTROLOGY 4 PURPOSE, POWER & PER:SPECTIVE**: *A Primer for the Seven Rays & the Work of Alice Bailey*
- **IN THE WORLD BUT NOT OF IT**: *Heaven, Hell & the Many Faces of Enlightenment & Ascension*
- **UNWINDING THE KARMIC WHEEL**: *The Journey from Survival to Compassion*
- **CORE VALUES**: *Recognizing & Surviving the Global Assault on Our Personal Autonomy*
- **UNCOILING THE SERPENT**: *Kundalini & the Dynamics of Spiritual Maturity*
- **SELF-WORTH**: *Its Origins, Faces & Remedies*

# Table of Contents

## THE I CHING - 52



## THE TAROT - 64



## MASTER NUMBERS - 78

## PUTTING IT ALL TOGETHER - 99



## APPENDIX - 121

# NUMEROLOGY

## *Life's Mirror of Vibration*

---

### INTRODUCTION

---

Through all my years in metaphysics I have come to understand that everything vibrates. That is, everything moves or breathes, to and fro, up and down, in and out, before and after, etc. Life, or energy, constantly pulses, cycles, moves and breathes. We perceive something as being alive simply by observing that it moves or breathes. How fast or slowly that occurs is something that we may perceive if it differs from our own speed of movement. For example, if we are driving on the road next to someone and they are moving at the same speed, we may not sense a difference between us as we appear stationary to each other. But if someone is passing us or we are passing them, we then notice a difference in our positions relative to each other. Suffice it to say that when we perceive vibration or movement that is different from ours that we are more likely to notice it simply because it *is* different. Numbers give us the ability to measure that difference but, more importantly, they give us a way to define or describe those differences. The study of recognizing those differences through varied movement of vibration is called numerology.

We can take this one step further in saying that because numerology allows us to discriminate differences that it is a vehicle for becoming aware of circumstances broader than what we are currently conscious of. That is, what we notice by way of those differences brings us to an awareness of the world that is much larger than our personal current focus. Numerology is a tool for *expanding* our awareness. The earliest sciences were mathematics and astronomy. Astronomy gave us the ability to "notice" measurable movement in the heavens and mathematics gave us the language to describe it. Numerology is a child of both.

My approach to using numerology is a bit different than most in that I approach what is the *potential* for our intelligent actions as being completely dependent on anticipating the circumstances and *using* our skill in making the best *choices*. That is, nothing is written in stone, fated or "destined" to occur. The circumstances that life presents us with are simply options for our choices. Our own capacity for depth and awareness are functions of our capacity to adjust our actions and perspective through making choices. Hence, everyone's "spiritual maturation" and personal growth will be completely individual and dependent on the choices that we make.

Generally, numerology books begin by giving us the meanings of numbers and then proceeding to personal applications. In light of the fact that most of us read with the intention of learning how people and situations compare to us, this will enable us to refine our self-image with ever deepening clarity. Most of us learn the feel and concept of things that apply to our own personal experience most easily. Because of this I prefer to give you numerological tools to make it personally relevant *first* so that the meanings you discover as you read will resonate more intimately and inclusively with your personal circumstances and experiences. These will help you to retain a more memorable "infusion" of meanings. Let's begin first with our *birth path* and the method to calculate it. I would suggest that you also figure those of the members of your family so as we go over the number meanings you will have practical examples in your family to make the meanings more personal and give you much more depth and relativity. This way you will see and feel the characteristics of each vibration come alive through your own family, friends and "enemies." Let's first start with the *birth path*.

# YOUR BLUEPRINT

## BIRTH PATH

Our *birth path* indicates the vibration or lesson that we were born under and that we are *learning to embody*. It's important to understand that our *birth path* does *not say who we are* but tells us the vibration that we have stepped into in order to *learn and grow proficient in its handling*. Like buying a different car, we must become familiar with its feel, size and capability before we can become proficient in its use. Only then will we learn its little quirks and advantages leading to the refinement of our ability to use it. One of the reasons that many numerologists and astrologers are able to assess a client's vibration or sign upon first meeting is that the qualities being worked on by the client have *not yet been refined or integrated* so they might blend in with the rest of their personality. When the vibration's characteristics have been fully assimilated and integrated, they will more often than not be undetectable. Let's move on to the math.

| |
|---|
| **1949 (Year)** |
| **10 (month)** |
| **19 (Day)** |
| **1978 (New Year)** |

**1+9+7+8 = 25 / 7**

If we take the year, month and day and add them up as in a math problem, we will arrive at a new year. Add the numbers in the new year and you will often receive a two-digit number. Add this two-digit number together to get a single primary digit. Retain all three numbers for future use.

Now, do this small calculation with everyone who is important to you, even your "enemies." The more people you have done this with, the more the next section will make sense to you. You will see the vibrational characteristics of each number come alive in the people you have done this with. But remember, these vibrations are *not who they are* but what they are struggling to *become by learning to be proficient in handling their path vibration.*

***One Birth Path*** – Essentially, you are on your own. You need to learn to develop without having to depend on others. There are no guarantees of support and no one will save you. You must become independent. There will be times that you feel very lonely, however, you will have all the freedom you need to do what you want to do. You are born to *learn* to be a leader by example *not* by telling others what to do. Recognition comes from within *not* from outside of yourself. You must speak up for what you want. People are not mind readers. Never assume anything. Verbalize. Have no expectations of others. Learn to initiate action. Trust yourself. Act on more than what you're sure of. Life is not security. Death & boredom are.

***Two Birth Path*** – Relationships and partnerships are at the core of your life lesson. You were born to learn to support others *and yourself*. If you seek the limelight, don't. You will be sorely disappointed. Someone will almost always step in and take it. You must mature past the need to take sides. Decide what is needed for all *including* yourself. To do only for yourself to the exclusion of others or vice versa corrupts the balance of things. Fix the problem *not* the blame. *Every* situation has two sides but you are not always required to choose or commit to one. Sometimes it's only there for you to simply observe. Understand that all life is comprised of duality so you may become aware of the larger scheme of things. Learn to listen. Learn to accept rejection. Rejection by others is only a reflection of their preference *not* a statement of your value in the universe.

Don't allow yourself to become be defensive or apologetic for your preferences.

***Three Birth Path*** – Some kind of instruction or education are of necessity for you either through school, training or on the job experience. The key is to expand your awareness and your abilities. Issues involving culture will always lead you to contend with bias, bigotry and prejudice…yours and/or others. Learn to become unconditional in your acceptance of people and their situations. This does not mean that you should let people do to you anything they want. You have the power to stay, say no or leave. Judge yourself by what you've done according to your own conscience. If you judge yourself by what others believe, preach or do, you will have to wear too many hats. Do it from the heart and let it go. Simply shoot for doing your best and letting it go. Avoid addictive substances or situations that foster control or the last word. You must learn to govern yourself and prevent runaway situations like addiction, gambling, obsession and more. You must learn when to put the brakes on. However, the urge to escape is very strong. Sometime it *is* necessary to stand your ground and face the issues. The key is to allow others to be themselves but not at your expense.

***Four Birth Path*** – The physical world and its connecting structures are your main concern. Life is work and mostly physical but you must learn the joy of creating your own solid foundation. Effort is necessary if anything is to be accomplished. It must also be *your* work *not* someone else's. Do not take credit for what others have done. You must develop your senses *and your intuition* with the understanding that life offers much more than just your five senses and that everyone else feels slightly differently than you. This does not make them bad people. This includes but is not limited to your senses. Tangible elements must be balanced equally. Tangible elements include physical, *emotional*, mental and *spiritual* components. Understand that everyone has a right to their opinion and to lead *their* lives in the way that *they* see fit, even if it doesn't align with what you think or believe. You must learn which hill you want to die on and when to use timing to deal with non-synthesizable situations or "disagreeable" people. Some parts of tradition *are* necessary, including those that are not yours! They not only provide tangible continuity but provide a baseline for measuring accomplishments.

*Five Birth Path* - Go with the flow. Resistance is futile. You will be absorbed! If you attempt to force your way or hold on to immovability, you will feel nothing but resistance, pain and frustration. Resistance causes pain. Going with the flow is exhilarating. You are here to learn to change and exchange…communication, energy, love, thoughts, etc. If you are insecure, you are growing and flowing and following your bliss. If not, you are stagnant, bored and feel as if life has left you behind. Learn to see both sides and discriminate according to your values but above all, be flexible and allow the movement.

*Six Birth Path* – Commitments and priorities are of paramount importance. To extract a commitment from others means that you must also live up to their expectations. If you look for someone to take care of you, *you* will inevitably end up taking care of them. Few people say what they mean or do what they say. If you want a job done right, usually, you must do it yourself. When you make a commitment, there exists someone who will *always* disagree with you. You are idealistic about your values. But you must ask yourself, are they really what you've been *taught* to believe or are they actually yours and a result of your own experience? Life for you is to follow *your* values with the courage of your convictions. You're learning about choices and being accountable for them *not* responsible. There's a big difference. Accountable means you must acknowledge and accept them. Responsible is where you believe that you must doing something about them based on the expectations of others.

***Seven Birth Path*** – Seven is all about detachment. It's a vibration which provides you with the need and the opportunity to disconnect. It initially is the person who finds themselves immersed in another person or situation so much that they lose themselves. As you pull yourself out of the emotional soup, you slowly learn to keep one foot on the dock and one foot on the boat at all times. You must learn to distinguish between *your* feelings and those of others. You are an emotional sponge, have difficulty finding yourself at first. It will also be necessary to overcome the tendency toward being hypersensitive. Eventually, you find yourself seeking more time alone than the average person simply in order to ground out the effects of everyone you've encountered. This allows you to become more conscious of your inner self. In this way you will learn to remain detached long and often enough that you are able to recognize and keep control over your own destiny. It takes a monumental effort to hear that little voice inside. When you do, follow it and don't stray. When you stray, you end up feeling like a cork on an angry ocean. The solitude behind listening enables the beginning of wisdom.

***Eight Birth Path*** – The key to *any* success is to learn organization, discipline and how to work within the existing structure on your own. It also pertains to learning how the repetition of patterns produces repeatable circumstances. You tend to find others' organizations and accomplishments to be a very tempting draw for you to move in on and "improve" upon. This causes tremendous resentment in others. Do your own work. When you do, you'll know that the accomplishment is your own and that it's clear that the credit is also. Ask yourself, who or what determines the authority in who you are, what you do and what you want. Are you following what you've been told to do or be or have you come to your own conclusions of what is important and what *you* believe is the "right thing to do?" The rules are meant to guide not restrict. When you work with others it blurs the line between your accomplishments and theirs. Eight is the number of cycles, karma and patterns. Learn to recognize when you are repeating a pattern…desirable or otherwise!

*Nine Birth Path* – There is a feeling that you must serve everyone who requests it of you. Although you have the profound ability to be many things to many people, it is not necessary to wear as many hats by being all things to all persons. Nine is also the end of a cycle and an invitation to let go which is also an intrinsic part of healing. Nine cleans out the closets by wrapping up and finishing up lingering issues. There is always a time where what you have been working at or on is at a point where all that can be done has been done. Granted you are a natural healer but you must also discriminate *when* to use your abilities or not and on *whom*. Just because you have a diversity of experience and interest doesn't mean that you must allow everyone else to use you and them nor are you responsible for their predicaments or their outcomes. Some people intentionally keep their difficulties and diseases for emotional security and some people need their diseases and difficulties to provide a karmic doorway to gain a new perception of themselves. You can be a facilitator but you're not responsible for them. No one needs you more than you.

---

## CRITICAL YEAR

---

The year that was arrived at in the previous example, 1978, is of additional importance. I call it your *critical year*. During this year the you will likely have had or will encounter some type of experience or personal change that changes the course of your life. It might be a move, a marriage, birth of a first child, traumatic experience, choice about career, or some other experience or choice that has or will have life path changing consequences.

The *critical year* may happen at any time in your life. It might happen in infancy or old age. So, now you may now be saying, "I was only three years old. What could I possibly decide?" However, it may be likely that your family made a move, lost a member of your family or maybe even adopted you. These changes could drastically change the course of what is expected for you. In this you can see that the circumstances may not always be the result of a personal choice. Sometimes your environmental conditions provide your "choice."

It may be that the *critical year* has not yet occurred. In this case it will be much harder for you to figure out the meaning of its future ramifications let alone what it might be that brings a major change about. In this case, the best you can do is be diligently aware of your choices and what occurs that might have a profound effect on how you live your life. I have found that "second guessing" or assuming what it actually is in such a case is almost never what we thought it might be until we assess its effects way down the line long after the occurrence or the choice has been made.

Lastly, I would like to add that your *critical year* will occur at the same time and vibration as one of your *personal years* which I will cover after we talk about their meanings.

## CYCLES & PATTERNS

*Vibration,* is a vehicle for change and exchange. It moves from one extreme to its opposite; day verses night, up verses down, etc. How fast or often that is done is calculated in a measured time frame, usually, called *cycles* per second, or even minutes, hours or any other measure of time. This speed at which this alternation of "sides" occurs is called the *frequency.* A complete "inhale and exhale," or peak and then valley, is considered one cycle. That is, a movement from one extreme to the other is called a *cycle.*

## THE ABSTRACT OF IT

Numbers were invented to mark measured segments of a cycle. For example, there are 360 points in a circle. There are eight phases in the moon cycle. There are seven (7) twenty-four-hour (24) periods in a weekly cycle. There are eight (8) points of reference in a musical scale and there are sixty-four (64) points in the cycle of Yin and Yang. Each *cycle* is divided into segments which, when numbered, tell you in which part of the *cycle* you are in; that is, how far from the beginning or end of that *cycle* you are and what quality of action or awareness is available to you at any of those given points. In the same fashion, numerology is segmented into nine (9) segments before returning to the starting point again. We count one (1) through nine (9) and then at ten (10) we arrive at a one (1) with a zero (0) attached signifying the *next cycle beginning* on through nineteen (19=1+9=10=1+0=1) ) and then on. Numerology is a measuring of movement through a *cycle* of actions with specific qualities and perspectives available at *each* of those points whether that be a musical note, day of the week or a numerical position. What's interesting about this is that every number has the same basic meaning and vibration no matter what part of the application they are found at, yet, are just interpreted from different perspectives as an extension of prior circumstances produced in prior *cycles*.

## THE TANGIBLE APPLICATION

Although the numbers themselves are abstract, their application is simple. Simply apply the numbers to any time frame that completes a pattern (*cycle*). You can do this from two perspectives. You can either take a time frame that matches the number order (use nine years for the one through nine sequence) or you can take a segment of time and divide it into the number order (take a circle of 360 and divide it into twelve equal segments as in astrological signs or houses). I will use the first example of nine years.

The parts that the overall pattern (*cycle*) are divided into nine (9) separate and consecutive years gives us the time span that each segment (one year) exists within the pattern or *cycle* of nine (9) years. So, as we move through the pattern, the first year will present characteristics of what the number one symbolism presents, the second year will present characteristics of what the number two symbolism presents, and so on. This will begin for each of us at birth with the number symbolizing our *birth path*.

For example, if we are born into a seven (7) vibration, as our *birth path*, we are also at the peak of a seven (7) *personal year*. At our first birthday we would be at the peak of our eight (8) *personal year*, at two (2), a nine (9) *personal year*, etc. The next year would begin a new nine-year (9) cycle. So, at four (4) then, we would be at the peak of a one (1) *personal year* in the new nine-year (9) cycle. In nine (9) more years, we will be at the peak of another new one-year (1). This will carry on throughout our lives, that is, following through nine-year (9) cycle after nine-year (9) *cycle*.

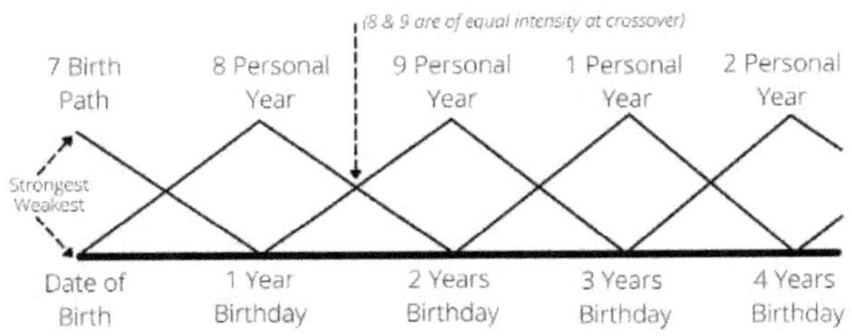


As you look at the diagram you can see that our native starts their life off at birth with the seven (7) vibration being the strongest and most prevalent. As we move on in time we can see that the seven (7) vibration begins to wane and the eight (8) vibration begins to gain in intensity. At birth plus six months we see that the seven (7) and eight (8) vibrations are of equal intensity. But as we pass that six-month point, we can see that the seven (7) vibration begins to wane and the eight (8) vibration grows in intensity until the first birthday where it becomes the strongest.

# PERSONAL YEAR

After gaining an understanding of these dynamic forces under our belt, let's take look at our *personal year* and what we can expect as we sojourn through each one of them. Remember, your *birth path does not change…*ever! The *personal year* adds a slightly different perspective the to the *birth path* lessons. Each year, starting with your base *birth path*, your *personal year* moves to the next segment of the current nine-year (9) cycle in terms of what we're exposed to, what vibrations we can use toward moving along on our *birth path* and what kind of situations we can anticipate dealing with during each year.

**2020 (Current Year)**
**10 (Birth Month)**
**19 (Birth Day)**

**2049 (Personal Year)**

**2+0+4+9 = 15 / 6**

To figure the *personal year* take the current year, month and day and add them up as in a math problem, we will arrive at the *personal year*. Add the numbers in the personal year and you will often receive a two-digit number. Add this two-digit number together to get a single primary digit. Retain all three numbers for future use.

Before we move into what each *personal year* might bring, it's important to understand that when we change from one *personal year* to another that it will likely happen very slowly and evenly throughout the year. Don't expect any changes to come along like we might throw a light switch. They may, but not likely. More likely they may change so gradually and we might not even realize a change is available, let alone, occurring. The slightest beginning of each year's vibration will commence starting six months before the birthday indicated for the current year. After peaking in intensity on the birthday the vibration will begin to diminish and continue to wane in influence for the six months following the current year's birthday.

*One Personal Year* – Personal one years almost always show physical manifestations of our new actions and decisions. We may change our career, have new child, acquire a new spouse, move to a new home, and many, many more subtle possibilities that we might not realize will or may have occurred until way down the line. In light of this we must take care that our decisions for new actions or ending old ones will be in the direction that we want. Understand that what we decide now may last for more than just for the upcoming nine-year cycle. The two-digit number will add depth and dimension to the simple single digit number arrived at. This will be covered later on in the book.

*Two Personal Year* – We must pay attention to our relationships. Relationship can mean person to person, person to job, person to environment or any way of relating that involves two or more people or situations. A two vibration is a function of awareness through opposition of positions, viewpoints or any aspect of separation. During this year we will receive feedback from others for what we have decided to do or not do in our new one year. This will bring us to a sorting of our friends and enemies depending on how they have reacted to our new choices and behavior following the new one vibration we've incorporated. Be supportive of others but not to the extent that you sacrifice your own health or welfare. Be satisfied to work from the background. Don't pick sides, just focus on what is important. The relationships will handle themselves as long as we listen and see and accept both sides of every situation.

*Three Personal Year* – Whatever you were unable to do or neglected to do in your one-year is now in a position to be revisited. Take the opportunity to tie up the loose ends of whatever has been left unfinished. It might not be as easy as it would have been in the one-year since some of the circumstances surrounding the issues have changed and solidified. You may have to do it a little differently but the opportunity to redo them is available now. After that you may expand into whatever area you wish. However, if you don't clean up the "leftovers" they will likely create interference for the new endeavors you wish to pursue. Once these potential impediments have been handled you can expand on those issues and others of your choosing. This expansion can take the form of going to school, advancing your career or adding to any other endeavor that has been started in you one-year. Additionally, new projects that have been effectively begun in the one-year now have an opportunity to be brought to a level well beyond the ordinary. It is now that they will be noticed by others. Be careful not to over-inflate them. No one likes a braggart.

*Four Personal Year* – This is a year to deal physically what you've begun in your one-year. Manifestation has taken shape. This is the time to work and set its foundation. Make sure that the effort you focus on leads to producing stability and usefulness. Flair and fanfare have no place now. This is the time for establishing the solid essentials. In the same vein, what you establish now will persist at least into your nine-year. Make sure that what you put in place now represents the endurance that you prefer. The majority of what you deal with this year will be tangible and interrelate with worldly issues. This is also a time for building health and setting patterns in place that will extend the physical performance and endurance of you and your projects. The scientific method will be a good tool to use this year.

*Five Personal Year* – Sit back and assess your creation. How can it be changed in order to improve its usefulness? What must you adapt? What must you give up? What must you strengthen? Talk about all sides. Be open-minded. Try new things. Go with the flow that your creation has led you toward or revamp it altogether. This is a year that communication is of the utmost importance. Exchanging with others, verbally, emotionally and physically has never been more important. As others understand what you are doing and why, there can be a plethora of insight available for you to use in order to improve and streamline your efforts. You will also find out how others feel about what your intentions are. This is not the time to "hold on." It is a time to look, listen and incorporate that which will make you more fluid and flexible. This is a time where you can see how the project you began in your one-year affects the people and environment around you. Notice what parts work and what parts create static. Allow yourself to make adjustments that make it better for you and the people you care about.

*Six Personal Year* – This will be a year of choosing where you will commit yourself based on your personal decisions, priorities and responsibilities. The first five years have shown you which issues and their activating factors would best apply to your newest and latest projects and insights and how they can validate how you live your life. Now that you have assessed your successes and failures thus far and decided where to go from here you must also have the courage of your convictions and the "stick-to-itiveness" to see it through. This will be in spite of whatever anyone else might think or say about you. You must also understand that whatever you commit yourself to there will *always* be someone who opposes you. This cannot be prevented and comes with the territory of choosing. This vibration crystalizes your values and shows them more clearly using your opposition as a reflection. On the heels of all this assessing, your self-image and how you want to come across to others will reveal itself. Money will do well for you but only if you have taken care of the appropriate commitments and responsibilities that lead to its earning. If your commitment and application to your values are absent, so will be the money.

*Seven Personal Year* – This is the year to go inside. The world will accommodate us by making people who were ordinarily abrasive seem to become much more intolerable. This is your Higher Self's way of making you withdraw in order to integrate your changes and to consider how your new accomplishments will change you as a person *internally*. This year is all about inner work. The down side is that it may bring loneliness. The upside is that if you've had a desire to study a subject of personal interest, learn self-improvement techniques, increase your personal proficiency in a particular skill or just take some time to get your environment into a more comfortable or orderly state, this is the time to do it. It's a time of meditation, reflection and *inner* study. This is not something that will observed from the outside by others. It's time to get your *inner* affairs in order. This is a great time for adding schooling or training. It's also a great opportunity to find the quiet time necessary to develop your intuition. In addition to finding abrasive people more so, your sensitivities will be heightened to an extreme state. One of the benefits will be that as you relax more into your quiet state, you will intuitively know where people's actions will take them simply by feeling and observing them. It can be a year of prophecy. Be careful of any toxic substances and reassess any regular medications. You will likely be oversensitive to both this year.

*Eight Personal Year* – This is a year of recognizing your personal patterns and either streamlining them or rearranging them if they have landed you in repeatedly difficult situations. You now see the fruits and the shortfalls of the last seven years of labor. This is a year of payback. Your successes will come back to reward you and your faults will come back to haunt you. If you have been responsible and organized you are likely successful. If not, you will feel the impact of the smack of a "big two-by-four upside your head" as a wakeup call if only just to get your attention! This is the beginning closure of this cycle where you are to recognize the positive and negative patterns and changes you've set in motion in your one-year and five-year. You must be accountable and take responsibility for their creation and their proper disposition. This is also a year where you adjust your perspectives concerning authority, that is, being it or responding to it. Generally, for most people, an eight-year is a year to reap and measure your successes and failures in handling the most recent cycle. Along with your six-year, this is another potentially good money year if you've acted appropriately.

*Nine Personal Year* – This is the "clean out the closets" year. You must release all influences that work contrary to your purposes including people, situations and patterns. This is also the beginning preparation for any new projects that you have in mind for the upcoming one-year. This is the vibration of dentistry, demolition and refurbishments. Anything that streamlines or dumps extra weight "lightening your airplane" for better flight fits the bill. Nine is also a medical vibration. In this way a nine-year is the best year for improving health by eliminating influences that bog you down or tie up your energy. Most illnesses are cause by blocked or inhibited energy flow throughout the body. This year you may feel that you must "fix" everyone's issues before your own. If you buy into this perceived obligation, you will be overwhelmed by needy people. This perceived obligation is also something which must be purged. Allow and encourage others to be accountable and responsible for their own situations. Show them how if you must but don't do it for them or you will become "the gift that keeps on giving." Learn how to streamline your life and teach others to do the same. If you don't cut any parasitic ties now, the hindrance and the resistance in the new cycle will be much more than the leftovers of what you could normally handle in the upcoming three-year.

## WHEN BIRTH PATH & PERSONAL YEAR COINCIDE

When the *birth path* and the *personal year* resonate to the same number, this year is a highly important point in each of our *personal year* cycles. Remembering that the *birth path* represents why we are here, every time the *personal year* resonates with it, it compounds its effects in terms of our life lessons and experiences. Relative to the nine-year cycle, we may even interpret its effects as being of equal importance to any of our personal one-years. We also know that one of those synchronized years will be our *critical year*. We know this to be a pivotal life experience.

Relative to vibrations, energies and intensity, when two or more numbers align, the sum of their influence will be much more than the simple sum of their parts. Any type of resonance has the effect of catalyzing the effects of each part so there is a constant augmenting of their overall effect. The end result will be individual as it will depend on how open we are to allowing it to freely resonate through us. Do we bury it or do we allow it free expression? Free expression is almost always the best path. Burying it almost always adds to our *shadow* and puts its effects out of our direct awareness and control. Then, it usually springs up unexpectedly at the most inauspicious times.

## IN A BROADER VIEW

Now that we've covered a good part of our personal meanings, I think we can now look at the broader meanings of the numbers without the little, "What about me?" voice jumping up and down inside and feeling left out in the background of our minds.

The numbers themselves, especially the single digits, have a much wider application than just to our daily lives and issues. Since everything vibrates, I think it's only fair to say that everyone and everything, from rocks to people, have a vibration that can be "labeled" with one of the single digits. To do this we just have to think in terms that are a bit more general.

Here we need our capacity for seeing things in an abstract perspective. That is, the meanings may not necessarily show us a concrete connection to how things are. We will need to move past our senses and allow our intuitive side to *feel* the vibrations from a more *in*tangible perspective. With this in mind, let's move on toward looking at the numbers from a more universal viewpoint. I will use words and phrases with occasional explanations to give you more of a *feel* for the numbers rather than something mental that you can itemize or chew on. Turn off the brain and let it "flow" over you.

*ONE - UNITY – CIRCLE -* Unity – Focus - Totality – Integrity - First – Solitary – Independent – All Inclusive – Beginnings - Complete Unity of Existence – Freedom – Alignment – Infinitely divisible - An amalgamation of parts which must have Integrity, Inclusiveness & Synergy

*TWO - DUALITY - YIN & YANG -* One in Terms of Halves – Opposition – Resistance – Perspective - Polarization within the One - Archetypical symbol of division – Relationship – Division produces discord – Parts of a unity – Separate from the source - Separates, divides and breaks up within unity – "Go forth and multiply" – Need of co-operation -

*THREE - EXPANSION – TRIANGLE -* Growth - One in terms of thirds - Pythagorean symbol of equilibrium – Man plus woman equals birth - Division by thirds - Procreation - Family – Acceleration – The Trinity – Triads - The pyramids – Ease of movement

*FOUR - FOUNDATION – SQUARE -* The physical world - Sacred to American Indians - Brahma had 4 heads, 4 Vedas and 4 Tantras – North, east, west and south - Symbolic of nature – Physical dimension - Arms of an open cross in which life takes place – Co-ordinates - Enclosure - Tradition – Work - Stasis

*FIVE - CHANGE – PENTAGRAM -* Communication - Exchange - Evolution - Pentacle - Davinci's upright human being - Healing - Five senses - Sanitation - Medicine - Five systems that compose the body – Discovery - Human order - Signets of Solomon

*SIX - DECISION – HEXAGON -* Priorities – Responsibilities – Commitment – Conflict – Self-concept – Discrimination - 6 Days of Creation - 6 Surfaces of A Cube - Genesis - Fruitful - Progeny - Commitment - Conflict

*SEVEN - REFINEMENT - 6-POINTED STAR* (Unity Of 2 Triads) - 7 musical tones – 7 colors – 7 days of the week – 7 chakras - 7 religions - 7 immutable universal laws – 7 planes of existence - Cosmic order - Detachment

*EIGHT - COMPLETION – INFINITY -* Time - Motion - Cycles – Infinity – Repetitive patterns - Snake with tail in Its mouth - Frequency - Time cycles - One becoming aware of itself through multiplicity - Days & nights of Brahma

*NINE - UNIVERSALITY -* Humanity – Clean out the closets – Restoration – Optimization – Demolition - Rehabilitation - Recovery - Perfection of all forms - Purification - Purging - Jack of all trades – Teach and learning by example

These meanings should give you a more general *feel* of what the numbers resonate and vibrate with. With a widened perspective under our belt, let's move on to another aspect of how they are applied.

# YOUR ARSENAL

Thus far we have talked about the vibration under which you are entering this life. In tangible terms, it is essentially hypothetical until you have experiences that illustrate the extent and quality of the choices that you make as a result of feeling and acting on those intangible vibrations. Essentially, your *birth path, your critical year* and your *personal years* all provide opportunities for choice and action that are aligned with the tasks and lessons you have accumulated through in past lives and need to work on in this life. When you incarnate, you are literally *pulled* into your new spiritual and practical environment through the attraction of the combined vibrational resonance of all your past life choices and actions. Consider it an overall matrix of coagulated conditions designed to elicit new awarenesses and perspectives through the choices available to you in this life.

Those vibrations that you are attracted toward and drawn into are those of your parents and their physical, emotional and mental heritage that match or repel, or a combination of both, your past life residue of "accomplishments." When I say residue, I refer to the unfinished experiences that were left incomplete in past lives. Your parents will now set the stage for your personal belief system and the life trajectory needed to actualize the new awarenesses and perspectives necessary for finishing your past life incompletes and moving toward your next level in your spiritual growth. As you incarnate, they will select a name for you which will reflect the physical, emotional and traditional heritage upon which *they* have lived and you will base this life's choices and actions on their history, either accepting them, rejecting them or simply moving on. Essentially, they will teach you how they want you to react to the world. This name will represent the arsenal and perspective that you will have to work with and through in addressing this life's lessons and growth.

So, simply put, what you *need to do* resonates to your *birth path, critical year* and *personal years* and what you *have to work with* is what your parents "give" you through your name, your upbringing and what they've trained you to believe or reject.

## WHAT'S IN A NAME?

Everything seen, heard, touched, tasted or smelled creates a vibration in the tangible world we perceive around us. A written or spoken name can be seen or heard by almost everyone. If we get close enough to others, we can include touch, taste and smell. These vibrations are what people get to know and remember about us. Our names, given or chosen, and our feels and faces are what people connect to their perception and memory of us. This now creates our presence in the world.

Our presence in the tangible world is what almost everyone has to work with. The many circumstances that this presence fills give us the life tools that we have at our disposal to carry out our life lessons. Our name resonates with our essence in the tangible world. When we analyze that name, we can determine what tools we have to work with. The names we have chosen or were given to us are comprised of letters, each having their own specific vibration. The combinations of these letters paint a picture of who we are perceived as and what we're capable of in the world. In short, our name(s) tell us what capabilities and stumbling blocks we may have and what available choices we may have in fulfilling our lessons.

## THE LETTERS

Each of the letters has its own vibration. The current system of assignation was established by Pythagoras of Samos in the fifth century B.C. in Greece. He established a secret school for initiates in Croton, Italy. His system replaced the Chaldean system founded in the sixth century B.C. in Babylon which did not include the use of the number nine as it was considered sacred and a symbol of infinity. In his system it is included.

| 1 | 2 | 3 | 4 | 5 | 6 | 7 | 8 | 9 |
|---|---|---|---|---|---|---|---|---|
| A | B | C | D | E | F | G | H | I |
| J | K | L | M | N | O | P | Q | R |
| S | T | U | V | W | X | Y | Z |  |

Our current day numerological system for our alphabet includes the digits one through twenty-six but can be reduced to the single digits of one through nine. I will cover the double-digit meanings later in this book, but for now, let's just examine the reduced single digits one through nine. This will keep it simple and give us the base numbers to work with while we work with our names. I will work with a fictional name just to learn how to use and interpret the numbers that each name vibrates to. Our fictional character will be John George Smith.

## THE EXPRESSION OR DESTINY

The *expression* or the *destiny* is how people perceive you. It is comprised of *all* the letters in the name. It manifests its vibration almost exclusively in the tangible world.

**John**
**1 6 8 5 = 20 / 2**

So, if the first name is John, and J=1, O=6, H=8 and N=5, then the total for the first name will be twenty or 1+6+8+5=20. Reduced, we get two (2+0=2).

**George**
**7 5 6 9 7 5 = 39 / 12 / 3**

The middle name is George. So, if G=7, E=5, O=6, R=9, G=7 and E=5, so the total for the middle name will be thirty-nine or 7+5+6+9+7+5=39. Reduced to a single digit will be three (3+9=12 then add again, 1+2=3).

**Smith**
**1 4 9 2 8 = 24 / 6**

The last name is Smith. If S=1, M=4, I=9, T=2 and H=8, and the total for the last name will be twenty-four or 1+4+9+2+8=24. Reduced to a single digit will be six (2+4=6).

So now, we add all three names together: 2 + 3 + 6 = 11 and reduce it further: 1 + 1 = 2. So, we now know that John George Smith's *expression* or *destiny* resonates to a two (2) vibration. This vibration is how the world will see John. It will also be how he feels himself in the tangible world. His *expression* or *destiny* is the *sum* of the qualities that he has at his disposal to manifest his life lessons. So, if we look back at the *birth path* meanings for the two (2) vibration, we can see the qualities that he *has* to work with. This does not necessarily mean that these qualities are developed, they may accrue throughout his life. But it *does* mean what is available to him, developed or not, to realize the *birth path* he has incarnated to work with.

So, what *do* we know about what John is seen as or capable of? Since two (2) is the number of relationships, John will be seen in *terms of* his relationships with others. That is, others will know him through comparison. John may even define himself in those terms. He will also be seen in how he supports himself and others. He will almost never be seen in the limelight and, more often than not, as working from behind the scenes. But, due to emotional development or its lack relative to the qualities of a two (2) vibration, his presentation and evolutionary state may be of a highly evolved quality or he may

```
  6      5 6    5     9    = 31 / 4
J o h n  G e o r g e  S m i t h
1 8 5 7    9 7   1 4  2 8 = 52 / 7
```

remain stuck in childish perspectives. In this, he may even waffle depending on the situations he finds himself in. He may be seen as a support to others or as being too selfish to contribute. Since the number two (2) is divisive, he may be seen as projective or, in the extreme, always pressed to find someone or something to blame for what doesn't turn out the way he prefers. He may be totally aware of his surroundings or totally obtuse to them. He may be easily fooled or blind to the obvious. He may be extremely helpful to others or play helpless to get others to cater to him. He may be overly defensive or apologetic as a function of diminished self-image or as a ploy for manipulation. The possibilities are endless and I think at this point you may be able yourself to draw many similarities to the people you know, evolved or not. As you learn the meanings and their possibilities, you will begin to develop your own internal "file cabinet" of numerical qualities and their manifestations. But enough about interpretation. Let's press on. The name is not flat or unidirectional. It has layers and divisions that further discriminate the qualities that we might be dealing with. We can also divide the name into vowels and consonants. Our diagram shows the vowels and consonants separately with their reduced totals. The vowels are open sounds and respond to aspiration. They are mostly energetic in nature and not easily recognized. They are boundless and have no limits. The vowels can be considered a representation of the *Soul's Urge* or *Secret Desire*. Conversely, the consonants respond to expiration and have hard sounds and manifest mostly in the physical and tangible world. Their expressions essentially "crystalize" themselves and have clearly specified boundaries. The consonants can be considered a representation of the *quiet self* or *personality*.

## THE QUIET SELF OR PERSONALITY

When we look at the *quiet self* or *personality*, we can see the qualities and abilities that John actually has at his disposal. The number we find summing up his consonants is seven (7). But seven (7) is very different from all the other single digits. To begin with, seven (7) is the only single digit number that doesn't divide evenly into the 360 degrees of a circle. Why is this important? Because the cycle, or its representative the circle, is the symbol of the repetitive movement of how all energy manifests in life. It begins and ends in the same place and has cleanly divisive points on the circle by every single digit other than seven (7). This tells us that all the other single digits have points of character that are easy for us to discriminate in the physical world. That is, they have qualities that be easily perceived by our minds because our mind needs to separate things so we can see and feel the borders of where they begin and end. For example, in six (6), we make decisions that we hold to or not. In eight (8), we either border it or free it. In two (2) we either push it or pull it. I think you get the idea. However, with seven (7) being not evenly divisible in the cycle, we really can't tell where it begins or where it ends, where it starts or where it stops. It's nebulous. Nothing is clear about it. This is how other people will perceive John's capabilities or debilities. Nothing clear about him. They never know whether he's coming or going, there or not. Seven (7) does not give a clear indication of his qualities. But you might say, but what about the days of the week? What about the musical scale; all the things that sevens (7) symbolizes? But tell me, where exactly does one day end and the next begin? Where does the frequency of one musical note end before the next is actually in tune with what we perceive as the next? Is it flat or sharp? All the other single digits have specific points in the circle that we can discriminate. But seven (7) does not. This is the thing that might puzzle people about knowing what John is capable of.

If you read back to the seven (7) *birth path*, these are the qualities that are exhibited through this digit. Now whether John has perfected the use of these qualities and perceptions remain to be seen. The use of seven (7) must be developed. Without specific points or qualities, this may likely be more of a challenge for John or anyone else.

So, at this point we can say that the *quiet self* or *personality* represent qualities and detriments that may be used by the native toward manifesting their destiny in their *birth path*. However, it is necessary to learn how to use them proficiently.

## THE SOUL'S URGE OR SECRET DESIRE

John's *soul urge* or *secret desire* is a four (4). On first glance we could say that John George Smith desires a stable foundation and to be well structured. But even though four (4) talks about tangibility and stability, the vowels speak more of a place that deals with preferred goals and wishes rather than their actual potential for tangible manifestation. With his *quiet self* or *personality* being a seven (7), this will be a difficult road to hoe. With his *soul's urge* or *secret desire* resting in having solid, tangible and well-defined objectives, his capabilities are comprised of elusive boundaries and undefined potential. The task will be much like trying to grab a greased pig. It will take many attempts and a lot of practice to get the two vibrations to work together effectively. This will certainly be a life task for him.

This may only represent part of the difficulty in synthesizing the two energies. As a general rule, many more people than not know what they *don't* want and are often oblivious to what they *do* want, let alone, what it would look like. Our world has been rapidly changing in life perspectives and most of our early training has been concentrating on telling us who we are not, what we need to be, what is socially acceptable and worst of all, what we *should* want. As a result of this kind of programming, most people haven't a clue about what they actually want. Ask anyone and they'll say, "to be happy" or "not to have to do or be so and so" or some kind of vague and non-definitive goals. Fifty years ago you could have asked a child, "What do you want to be when you grow up?" Most would have said something very tangible and concrete like a fireman or policeman, movie star or a millionaire.

So, what does this mean to John and most people now? It means that most of us are largely unconscious of what our desires truly are. We've been programmed by the outside world and have no idea who we are, let alone, what we want. Looking at our *soul's urge* or *secret desires* should give us some recognizable idea of what it is that we truly want in our core. We just have to resist accepting what we're told that is by others. Our *soul's urge* or *secret desires* are representative of the small voice within that we usually can hear when the din from the outside world has been reduced to a minimum. It's like hearing a whisper in a crowded room.

So, our *soul's urge* or *secret desire* is a preferred existence that we are, at the least, unclear about, yet, it has a tremendous subconscious effect on the use of our abilities and detriments. It can either catalyze our efforts or sabotage our attempts. What John can utilize toward his path remains to be seen. Only his experience will tell.

## FIRST, MIDDLE & LAST NAMES

We can further apply specific meanings and perspectives to each of our names. Traditionally, most of us have a first, middle and last name that we can ascribe meanings to. Each offers perspectives and characteristics that we can discriminate depending on the "modality" that we are addressing. However, a small percentage of us were not given middle names. I will address that shortly.

Our names can be further divided into our first, middle and last. They can be interpreted where the first name relates to our physical self, the middle name relates to our emotional self and the last name relates to our traditional heritage as perceived through our spiritual mission. These can be considered the most dominant "modalities" that we usually deal through in our daily lives. We can further break *each* of these down also into their own *expression, soul's urge* and *quiet self*. But let's not get ahead of ourselves. Let's slowly examine the implications of each name. I will keep this simple but there is a wealth of perspectives that can be had by examining each name that we've either been assigned or chosen.

---

## FIRST NAME

---

*Soul's Urge*
**6** = **6**
**J o h n** = 6+5 = **11 / 2**
**1   8 5** = **5**   *Expression*
*Quiet Self*

Our first name is how we relate to the physical world. It represents physically what we do (*quiet self*), what we want (*soul's urge*) and how we appear to others (*expression*). It is the name of which we are the most conscious. John's first name *soul's urge* is six (6), his *quiet self* is five (5) and his *expression* is two (2).

We can see with the *soul's urge* of six (6) that John wants to have commitment, stick-to-itiveness and consistent values. Yet, in his "tool box" or his *quiet self* he has the changeability and flexibility of the five (5). What might be even more difficult, and depending on his emotional maturity and awareness, he may not even be conscious or aware of wanting stick-to-itiveness and consistent values. His conscious actions and unconscious influences may push him in two different directions, effectively but initially, sabotaging himself. Only gradual work and experience with and in the new vibrations may bring him to a point where he has learned to use this particular combination. In this way incarnation is much like a person who has been put into a different type of automobile different from what they've been accustomed to in a past life, aka, the physical vehicle they are now working with is different and will take some getting used to.

# MIDDLE NAME

*Soul's Urge*

```
 5 6      5 = 16 / 7
G e o r g e          = 12 / 3
 7     9 7  = 23 / 5    Expression
```
*Quit Self*

Our middle name relates to our feelings and emotions. The *soul's urge* for John's middle name is seven (7), the *quiet self* is a five (5) and the *expression* is three (3). So, John's emotional *soul's desire* is to have detachment, refinement and sensitivity. He might not be aware of this. If he is, he will know how to handle the duality and changeability that the five (5) gives him the potential to use. His communication about his feelings may be focused and well grounded. If not, he will likely get caught up in the grosser vibration of the polarized minutia inherent in the five (5) vibration. Concurrently, and if he *has* become mature and experienced enough, the five (5) representing his "tool box" or *quiet self* will provide him with a conscious capability for emotional flexibility. He will first have to determine what emotional refinement and sensitivity looks and feels like so that the flexibility of the five (5) will give him recognition of the range of choices for action, or inaction, available to him. The three (3) *expression* will produce the expectation of an expansive emotional capacity in the people who have come to know him. That will take the form of either a mature life approach through remaining grounded and being able to handle emotional issues where others are concerned *or* he may subject to fits or meltdowns from being unwittingly thrown off by prevailing and changing emotional currents.

## TOO MANY OR NOT GIVEN A MIDDLE NAME?

This may be distressing to someone who was not given a middle name. On first glance we might feel that our family deprived us of an emotional expression when they named us. But consider this. If in past lives we were so emotional that it overpowered our lives, our attracting vibration through incarnation would be to bring us to a space where that emotional component might be minimized. I believe that this would bring us toward being open and balanced in approaching any emotional issue so as to not allow it to influence the effect of the other names. Effectively, there would be no emotional "bias" in dealing with life issues. This person might even *seem* emotionless to others.

Conversely, cultures like the Spanish and the Italians may have *many* middle names connecting to different people in their heritage assuring that full family influence applies to their feelings and emotional content. In these cases their prior incarnations may have been concentrated on other physical or mental development and almost absent of any feelings requiring a super influx of emotional influence.

The possibilities and reasons for added or absent middle names are endless. Have an open mind. No one has been deprived or extra-gifted. These things follow a very strict set of universal laws. There are very simple reasons for our seemingly "fated" naming. We simply may just not be aware of them. Make no assumptions.

## SURNAME OR LAST NAME

The last or surname represents our *family heritage* and *spiritual mission*. These represent the family dynamics that produce our perspectives in handling the people closest to us and the early environments that we are brought up in. This frames our life perspective for what we resist, what we yearn for, how we approach others and what we expect from our family and the rest of the world. If we are abused, we will come to expect abuse and potentially become abusers ourselves. If we have been raised to have respect (for ourselves and others), *Self-Trust* and encouragement, we will grow to give and expect the same from the world. The last name *expression* will generally be how others see our family through us.

Soul's Urge
9 = 9
Smith = 24 / 6 (*Expression*)
1 4  2 8 = 15 / 6
Quiet Self

For John's last name, his *soul's urge* is nine (9), his *quiet self* is six (6) and his *expression* is six (6). His family and heritage have taught him to focus on values, decisiveness and commitment. This will either be the result of direct training of these qualities or his family's neglect or abuse of them. If he was accepting of their training, he will be strongly invested in giving and getting commitments and basing his decisions and choices on what he has been trained to feel the need to be committed to. If not, he will feel the need to escape them and/or adamantly diminish their effects on him. His desire or *soul's urge* of nine (9) will be to either honor or repel *all* people and the commitments that they might imply. He will feel stressed by the need or urge to handle *everyone* who comes into his sphere of existence. Remember, nine (9) imparts the feeling that it is the person's responsibility to do for and respond to *everyone*. If his upbringing has prepared him in how to choose what he feels is important, his *quiet self* six (6) will enable him to scale down the urge to only what is absolutely necessary. His *soul's urge* and family experience will likely give him the desire to become a healer of some sort or someone who refurbishes people, situations or things.

# MARRIAGES, ADOPTIONS AND CHANGED LAST NAMES

One of the biggest questions asked when we talk about surnames or last names is what happens whether a spouse takes their partner's last name or not? The answer depends on how is it taken. Is it hyphenated? Is their own last name dropped and the spouse's is taken on? Do they keep their own last name? These choices can cause perspective differences by way of culture, religion, diet, lifestyle and much more. There are three distinct choices.

The traditional way is for the woman to drop her last name and take on her husband's. Essentially, this represents a traditional dominance of a patriarchal lineage and will require her to reflect and exhibit the traditions of her husband's family. Needless to say, when we add the total name together, the overall *soul's urge, quiet self* and *expression* will most likely, all be different and devoid of her own family influence. However, we must also remember that, at the least, twenty years of her persona will have already been formed under her maiden name. This will present tremendous pressure to change in the way she deals with family structure and discipline. This will also compound any disagreements between her and her mother-in-law, especially, if there are emotional imbalances between her husband and his mother.

If her last name is kept and hyphenated to the adding of her husband's last name, there will certainly be disagreements in the traditional line of issues, but the woman will not feel as much pressure to abdicate her own traditions and beliefs about family. She will feel more comfortable in keeping most of her twenty-year acquired identity. This will allow her to feel that she can let much of the patriarchal family pressure slide because she won't feel as if her total family identity is being invalidated. Then, she will be okay with some compromise. The inclusion of her own family name's *soul's urge* and *quiet self* will make this possible.

If she keeps her maiden name or prior married name, she will likely never fully be accepted by the husband's family. This will imply a rejection of the husband's family traditions. This, putting her on an equal footing with the matriarch of her husband's family, will create an unending conflict, if not an undercurrent, with the way her husband's family deals with family issues and requirements. The exclusion of her husband's family *soul's urge* and *quiet self* will only serve to verify this.

It must be understood that the extent of all these family conflicts and undercurrents are very much dependent on the emotional maturity of both families. If both families are fairly emotionally mature, there will likely be minor difficulties in adjustment. If there are emotional insecurities in either or both families, these issues will be exacerbated by the addition of a family "interloper" through marriage.

Adoptions may produce a very different kettle of fish. Many adoptions occur close to infancy. Because the original given name has not yet gained much traction, there will likely be minimal adjustment required if any. The older the child becomes; the more conflict is likely to occur.

In many adoptions even the first name is changed. This will follow reason because the child's total physical environment is usually changed. The results of this may not be immediately seen. When the child is born and given a name, the given names reflect how the child is perceived by the family he or she is born into. It also reflects how that family will have treated them. This translates to how their health, diet and caring has previously been applied. Depending on how late an adoption occurs, physical and emotional patterns develop that reflect the influence of the woman and her family who give them up for adoption. Close to infancy, the child will have not yet developed any verbal skills. As a result, physical and emotional patterns will be etched into the child with no mental comprehension on the part of the child. This may cause some emotional or physical patterns and tendencies that will be difficult, if not impossible, to assess and deal with in later years. The longer the first family has influence over the child, the more the child will have to compromise their identity relative to the two sets of *soul's urge, quiet self* and *expression* in later years.

## NICK-NAMES, CHOSEN NAMES & EXTRA NAMES

It's important to understand that simply because the numbers are present by virtue of the assigned or chosen name, the person may neither be aware of what they are capable of let alone be able to use what they have been "assigned" by their family. Our person may be younger than puberty and have no clue about what they're working with or why. Or we might have an older person whose stubbornness over life has never permitted the influences available to have taken effect.

As with many children, we also must consider that the child may have a given name like John but be

*Soul's Urge*

```
  6        = 6
J o h n      = 6+5 = 11 / 2
1   8 5 = 5        Expression
Quiet Self
```

*Soul's Urge*

```
  6        9 5 = 20 / 2
J o h n n i e        = 12 / 3
1   8 5 5     = 19 / 1   Expression
Quiet Self
```

called differently with a "nick name" by their family and friends such as Johnnie. In this name the *soul's urge* would be a two (2), the *quiet self* would be a one (1) and the *expression* would be three (3). This is quite a different combination of vibrations. This would create tremendous confusion for the child. To begin with, early on the family and friends would perceive him as a three (3) vibration. The two (2) *soul's urge* in "Johnnie" would pressure him into cooperating with what the family would *assume* he wants in conflict with the six (6) *soul's urge* in his given name which, incidentally, would pressure him into wanting to  make *his own* decisions in concert with what the world would expect of him. The family would also treat him as if he were a three (3) *expression* expecting him to be gregarious, effusive and expansive while his given *expression* would likely express as a two (2) desiring cooperation, partnership and working behind the scenes.

"Nick names" that are imposed on someone not only create problems for the person or child but even people who assign themselves "nick names" will likely be adding a vibration different from their given names causing some confusion in initiating their identity perception.

It is often that people will assign or choose names for themselves that might be evasive of the qualities that they might need to work with. For example, our prior example of John George Smith may choose to use his middle name, George, as his first name wanting to put his emotional self forward to people. This would, essentially, over-emphasize his emotional nature at the expense of his physical nature. He might choose to do this if his physical experience as a child had produced some difficult or harmful circumstances.

For others, if a different name is chosen or added, identity and lifestyle changes will likely apply whether the individual is aware of what and how they've actually changed. Some people may be unconscious of the implications and simply like how the name change makes them feel. Others may change their names consciously as they believe specific results may occur as a result of it. This often occurs when their emotional need often overpowers their understanding of the full effect of what they are actually doing. They know that this will change how they are perceived by others but often are unaware of the other issues the new names may bring to them. It changes how they are perceived by others and how they feel about what they want but doesn't change the abilities provided by their original *quiet self* to any extent until they build enough experience with the new name.

Changing one's name must be done with care and deep consideration about the effects that the new name will bring to us and *what we may be losing* by abandoning the original name.

## OUR "INITIAL" PERSPECTIVES

How we approach the use of our names can be seen by virtue of the first letter of each of our names. Much like beginning any task, we will have a tendency to use the tool which appears to us first in the tool box and likely the one we are the most familiar and comfortable with. This first letter of each name is the tool and is called the name's *capstone*. It is what initiates the action or "current flow" through the name that we will follow through when physical, emotional or heritage issues are activated. As per our example of John George Smith, when he deals with physical issues, the first name John will be activated.

Because the name starts with a "J" which is a one (1) vibration, he will approach physical issues initially as an independent actor preferring to act alone. He will also likely find himself being left alone by others and find that help may not even be available if it is needed or preferred. Once the one (1) has been initiated he will move on to the six (6) of choice and commitment, (letter "O"), then to the eight (8) of organization and structure, (letter "H") and then to the five (5) of communication and flexibility, (letter "N"). All the physical issues he encounters will follow this sequence of action, vibration and perspective and be initiated with the one (1) with follow-through every time he starts a new physical focus or begins a "second cycle" on the same issue. The other names will proceed the same way.

When dealing with the middle name," representative of feelings and emotional issues and beginning with "G," his first approach and reaction will be with the sensitivity of the seven (7), followed by each next letter and its corresponding quality in sequence.

The last name will follow the same process. The "S" will begin the process relating to family and traditional issues with the one (1) and move on through the letters respectively. We will analyze *capstones* a little more closely after we examine the double digits that each vibration reduces from. They have more attending characteristics which will give each letter a more detailed and colorful focus.

Thus far we have only spoken of the basic single digits that give only the most rudimentary qualities that a number might express. I have reduced double digits to keep things simple so as not to overload you with the necessity of learning more detailed representations on the onset of our journey. But now that you have a basic understanding of the numbers, it's important to know that *all* numbers and their sequence are important and that each letter is like a person with many characteristics and alternative ways of expression. As an example, we can look at the double digits fifty-three (53) and thirty-five (35). Both reduce to eight (8) and both relate to a type of cyclic growth but the fifty-three (53) initiates that growth through the communication and exchange of the five (5) and the thirty-five initiates that growth through the expansion and broadening of the three (3). This type of subtlety is what allows the double digits their independent coloring.

There are many sources that double digits can gain their representative meanings from but there are only two sources that I will use in any detail: the *I Ching* and the *tarot*. Both are considered divinatory systems. The *I Ching* is an ancient Chinese cyclic set of sixty-four (64) symbols depicting the natural cycle of life and the stages and options at which growth and evolution occur. Both of these sources utilize a science of progression and interrelationship and are eminently available to our intuition and applicable as a function of our awareness. The *tarot* is an ancient Egyptian set of seventy-eight (78) image imbued cards that were given meaning and structure to train people about life through a pictorial analogy, much like parables, for those who might not have had the mental capacity to process conceptual and abstract thought. Let's first take a look at the *I Ching*.

# THE I CHING

Most people are familiar with the Chinese yin and yang. Yin and yang represent all the sets of opposites known throughout the world as the primary exhibitor of duality. That duality exists within the Tao. The Tao can be compared to the western concept of God or the *All* which encompasses all things. One of the biggest differences is that the west personifies the concept of a god and the east does not.

So, the Chinese say that the physical world is constructed in terms of opposites. There are dark and light, up and down, before and after, with or without or any concept or perspective that can effectively be seen or felt in terms of opposites. These opposites and the movement between them make us aware of

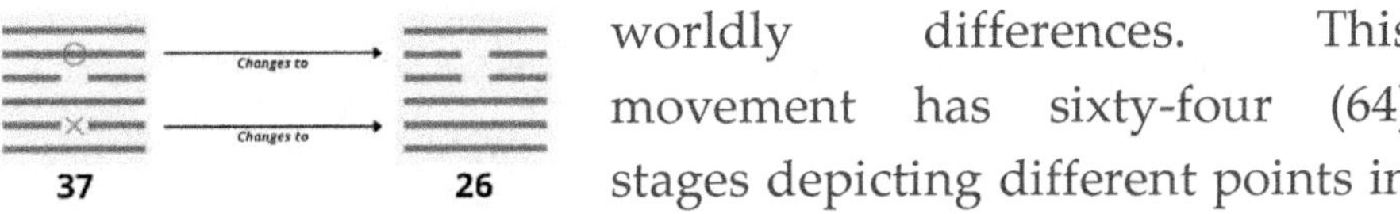


worldly differences. This movement has sixty-four (64) stages depicting different points in the completion of a full cycle of change. Each of these points is represented by a *hexagram* composed of six lines that are either yin, yang or in the process of changing between each other. If any of the lines are changing, as in the diagram, it will resolve to another hexagram depicting the qualities of the of the next progressive point in the movement of energy. When reduced, we can also see the change in single digits from a one (1) to an eight (8).

Unlike the west who sees most everything in black and white, the Chinese see life as a series of gray areas between the extremes moving from black to white and back again. These *hexagrams* each have a slightly different quality and perspective that represent the many points of in change and perspective that we and our energy go through as we evolve. Each of these *hexagrams* can be represented by a single or two-digit number.

| | | | |
|---|---|---|---|
| 1 The Creative | 17 Following | 33 Retreat | 49 Revolution |
| 2 Natural Response | 18 Decay / Repair | 34 Great Power | 50 Cosmic Order |
| 3 Difficult Beginnings | 19 Approach | 35 Progress | 51 Shocking |
| 4 Inexperience | 20 Contemplate | 36 Eclipse | 52 Meditation |
| 5 Patience | 21 Reform | 37 Family | 53 Developing |
| 6 Conflict | 22 Grace | 38 Opposition | 54 Subordinate |
| 7 The Army | 23 Splitting Apart | 39 Obstacles | 55 Zenith |
| 8 Unity | 24 Returning | 40 Liberation | 56 Traveling |
| 9 Restrained | 25 Innocence | 41 Decline | 57 Gentle Penetration |
| 10 Conduct | 26 Potential Energy | 42 Benefit | 58 Encouraging |
| 11 Peace | 27 Nourishing | 43 Resolution | 59 Dispersion |
| 12 Stagnation | 28 Critical Mass | 44 Dynamic Action | 60 Limitations |
| 13 Brotherhood | 29 The Abyss | 45 Assembling | 61 Insight |
| 14 Sovereignty | 30 Synergy | 46 Advancement | 62 Conscientiousness |
| 15 Moderation | 31 Attraction | 47 Adversity | 63 After the End |
| 16 Harmonize | 32 Enduring | 48 The Well | 64 Before the End |

As you can see in the preceding chart, each of the *hexagrams* embody a different quality or perspective that can be applied or addressed to any facet of our labeling in numerology. This is why I asked you to retain the double-digit numbers we arrived at when figuring the *birth path, personal years, critical year* and names. The depth of coloring and understanding that can be gained by reading the *I Ching* and *your* corresponding numbers is phenomenal. One of the best books I have found for this type of content is *The I Ching Workbook* by R.L. Wing (1979).

1949 (Year)
10 (month)
19 (Day)
1978 (New Year)

1+9+7+8 = 25 / 7

With this in our toolbox, let's take another look at John George Smith's *birth path*. John's *birth path* is a seven (7) coming from a number twenty-five (25). We know that the seven (7) is about detachment and we know that the main focus for him is to learn to "unhook" from his tendency to become immersed in the emotional needs and wants of other people. We add to the depth of the vibration through the derivation of seven (7) from the number twenty-five (25). The twenty-fifth *hexagram* in the *I Ching* speaks about *innocence*. The dictionary describes *innocence* as being "blamelessness and free of guilt or moral wrong doing." The *I Ching* talks about using the purity and blamelessness that the naivete of the *innocent* might have and applying it as a vehicle for disconnecting from emotional influences. But the *I Ching* also warns that this *innocence* must be honest, come from the heart and not be a contrived or untruthful claim emanating from the need to protect the security of our ego.

When a child is incarnated into an environment in which they are trained to believe that they are responsible for the feelings of others in their family, it becomes almost impossible for them to disconnect enough from the wants and needs of those others in order to focus on their own wants, needs and stability. This usually comes from a family member(s) who is, for the most part, insensitive to the needs and wants of others, especially their children, and assumes that they are there to be responsive to *their* needs and wants. A narcissistic parent is often the culprit. That parent will usually use very logical but coercive reasoning in convincing the child that it is *their* responsibility to cater to *their* moods. The child knows no better and is *incapable* of the common-sense reasoning required that would absolve them of the responsibility for accommodating the narcissistic parent at their own expense. One of the coercive factors in maintaining this perspective is the potential withholding of love by the parent if the child doesn't accommodate their spoken or inferred needs, wants and expectations. This feeling of needing to be accommodating gets transferred to the world and the growing child becomes hypersensitive to the needs, wants and expectations of others. They will either rebel or cave in to the expectation. This, then, becomes a major block to their own development. Yet, it hones their sensitivities to well beyond what the average person is capable of. The major task now is to regain their own emotional balance free of their overwhelming empathy for an emotional pressure coming from others.

*Innocence* as described in the *I Ching* tells us to hold to our values and experience of what *we* know to be true. Except for the fear of withheld love or recognition, no coercive reasoning will convince us that the ills of others are a result of our inability or refusal to cater to their preferences. Maintaining a sense of *innocence* is part and parcel toward accomplishing the detachment needed toward sustaining our own spirit's energy and integrity.

Seven (7) is a major numerical participator in the emotional maladies that many people in the "helping" fields such has nursing, social work and other "helping" professions are afflicted with. These are the people who become overly embroiled in becoming responsible for the welfare of others at their own expense. They have been fooled, usually by narcissistic parents, into believing that their "goodness" depends on how much they sacrifice for others. Developing a sense of innocence is a major tool for diminishing this delusion. Let's now take a look at the name.

## THE I CHING & THE NAME

Soul's Urge
6 = 6
**J o h n** = 6+5 = 11 / 2
**1   8 5** = 14 / 5   *Expression*
Quiet Self

Let's first take a look at John George Smith's first name. For his *soul's urge* there will be no change since there is only one vowel with a total of six (6). Stick-to-itiveness and commitment are still part of what he wants whether he is conscious of it or not. However, his *quiet self* and *expression* both have numbers that are derived from double digits. The five (5) of the *quiet self* comes from a fourteen (14) and the two (2) of the *expression* comes from an eleven (11). These double digits add a little color and detail.

The fourteen (14) in the *I Ching* talks about *sovereignty* and the proper use of power. John's *quiet self*, which represents change and flexibility, would likely still cause a bit of friction with the six (6) of his *soul's urge* but the fourteen (14) leading to the five (5) gives a better twist on how things might work out. The fourteen (14) *quiet self* has a very strong inherent balance of flexibility and as long as John doesn't allow his two (2) *expression* to degenerate into becoming mouthy, argumentative or contentious, which is its immature side. The fourteen (14) behind the five (5) will inspire trust and confidence from his family that he will do the "right thing." The moment John will lean into the "tit-for-tat" side of the two (2), that trust and confidence in him will vanish and the *sovereignty* of the fourteen

(14) will lose its potential. In this light, let's look closer at eleven (11) in John's expression.

We do know that John's two (2) *expression* could be argumentative and contentious because of the opposing quality present in the two (2). But the eleven (11), which the two (2) derives from, provides a different potential available to John. In the *I Ching* the eleven (11) is a number of *peace* or prosperity. So, if John can lean into the feeling of contentment or *peace*, which the eleven (11) makes available, the need to express the contentious part of the two (2) will be absent and the rapport with his family will remain calm. This will enable him to sustain their assumption that he is strong enough and trustworthy enough to "do the right thing."

With this explanation of the first name alone we can see that the name itself is a working dynamic that is subject to the maturity and choices of its bearer. If John reverts to contentiousness, it will cause one type of rapport with his family and if he moves into the more subtle and specific vibration of the double digits, things might turn out very differently. The trick for John is to recognize and use these differences knowing and understanding that these subtleties are within the reach of his potential growth, especially, since his *birth path* is a twenty-five (25) over seven (7) (detachment through innocence).

With these influences prevalent in only John's first name and its *physical* dimensions, let's move on and see what more we can deduce from his middle or *emotional* name.

         *Soul's Urge*
**5 6**    **5 = 16 / 7**
**G e o r g e**     **= 12 / 3**
**7**   **9 7**  **= 23 / 5** *Expression*
       *Quit Self*

From the diagram we can see that all three components of the name derive from a double-digit number. This adds a lot more color and specificity to how John's emotional disposition will integrate.

The seven (7) vibration of the *soul's urge* will impel John toward finding refinement and sensitivity. The fact that it derives from the sixteen (16) might throw a monkey wrench into actually acquiring it. The *I Ching* tells us that sixteen (16) is all about following the path of least resistance in the environment around us in order to achieve any peace. This can occur in one of two ways; either he can allow the emotional content of his surroundings to unfold on its own while he remains detached or he can submit to pleasing others just to keep a quiet and stress-free environment. The five (5) of the *quiet self* gives John the flexibility and intellect to deduce what is actually needed to establish that peace. The *I Ching* supports that with twenty-three (23) which talks about splitting apart. If John allows the chips of the emotional environment to fall where they may (23) and he remains detached from a security oriented emotional investment (7), the expanded nature of the three (3) *expression* will take precedence. If he does submit to a security oriented emotional investment by trying to control the environment, the twenty-three (23) will take precedence and everything will fall apart anyway holding him in a stagnant (12) emotional *expression*. It is in John's best interest to remain emotionally detached (7) if he wishes to keep the expansiveness of the three (3) of his middle name's *expression*. The minute he becomes invested or attached to the outcome, he becomes stuck in the momentum of his attempt to control the outcome. Let's move on to the last or surname.

The last name or surname is where the framework for his attitudes will be shaped by his family. That is, the traditions, physical, emotional and mental that his family exposes him to will set the stage for how he perceives and integrates with the world at large. It will also set his preferences for the types of people he will wish to attract and those who he will wish to avoid.

```
                Soul's Urge
     9      = 9
Smith                = 24 / 6
                       Expression
1 4   2 8 = 15 / 6
            Quiet Self
```

One of the first things we will notice is that John's last name's *quiet self* and *expression* (6) are the same. This will tell us that choices, commitments and priorities are at the root of John's family traditions. This is motivated by a *soul's urge* (9) to "fix" everyone as prescribed by the family's values (6). If the family is emotionally balanced, this will promote the servicing of others in a grounded and reasonably tempered progression of service. If the family emotional structure is off, insecurity will prevail and this servicing of others (9) will become exaggerated as an expectation and validation of his personal worth (6) by everyone connected to the family. How well John aligns with these values, balanced or not, will be the measure of how they treat and perceive him. John's first name *soul's urge* (6) resonates with the family's *quiet self* (6) and *expression* (6). This suggests that he will feel that it will be necessary for him to physically do things (first name's *soul's urge*) in alignment with the family's values in order to be accepted and included as one of them. If the family emotional balance is off or insecure, this will pressure him into an alignment with unhealthy attitudes toward chosen values. If the family *is* emotionally balanced, things will flow smoothly provided John acts in an emotionally balanced way himself.

John's family has the *ability* to be emotionally balanced through their *quiet self* (6) as derived from the *I Ching* hexagram of *moderation* (15). *Moderation* gives the family the potential to take the middle path when it comes to their *traditions* and *spiritual heritage*. As long as the family remains emotionally balanced, *moderation* will be at the basis of all issues that come to the forefront. Either way, John's *soul's urge* of his first name (6) will be a draw that keeps him connected to the family whether balanced or not.

His family *expression* is also a six (6) but derives from the number twenty-four (24) in the *I Ching* which is called *returning*. *Returning* talks about keeping things simple and *returning* to the most rudimentary form of whatever is being expressed. Generally, when we are in a family setting, many of the rapports expressed between the members of the family have all sorts of secrets, issues, fears and personal concerns that can be very convoluted and complicated. *Returning* brings us back to the most elementary and impartial factors that compose any situation in an attempt to simplify it. In a balanced family rapport, this will be a boon and a stable place for any of the family members to be. In an unbalanced family, many members will either create tremendous personal conflict, manipulate others or attempt to escape.

```
  6         5 6     5      9     = 31 / 4
John George Smith = 11 / 2
1 8 5 7     9 7   1 4   2 8 = 52 / 7
```

Lastly, we have the whole name of John George Smith to look at. The full name contains the most tangible of all the vibrations as it is what the world sees before they get involved with us to any depth. It is the broadest focus of our identity in the world. For John, this is a *soul's urge* of four (4), a *quiet self* of seven (7) and an *expression* of two (2).

With a *soul's urge* of four (4), the world might perceive that John would like to feel a solid connection and groundedness with well-established families, businesses and personal relationships. Solidity and security are what would appear to be his most obvious goal to the casual observer. This would also be observed if John followed the habitual detachment offered by a seven (7) *quiet self* removing him from any social chaos that might disturb that groundedness. They might even see his "escape" as a tendency toward being hypersensitive to his surroundings.

The thirty-one (31) that the four (4) *soul's urge* derives from talks about the *I Ching* and the *attraction* that is possible through being aligned and in sync with whatever force represents that groundedness and solidity. So, in order for John to accomplish that solid sense of security he must be sure to align himself with what he wants to be part of. So, for a relationship he must be aligned with his partners values, likes and dislikes. For a business he must be in keeping with the rules, goals and policies of the company. For a family, he must align with their traditions and social expectations.

The seven (7) of his *quiet self* accomplishes his inner peace from a different angle. The seven (7) derives from fifty-two (52). In the *I Ching* the fifty-two is referred to as *meditation* or keeping still. So, when John removes himself from a chaotic or toxic situation it enables him to center himself and to shut down from being affected by any outer influences. We often find the seven (7) present in the *quiet self* in people who have trouble with turning down the volume on who and what they empathize with. Not having a defense against unwanted emotional immersion is an extremely debilitating occurrence for people who have highly developed receptivity. We see this in artists who seem eccentric because they have a need for privacy and being alone in what appears to be the extreme. John will feel very much the same.

Lastly, John's two (2) *expression* marks his most obvious presentation to the world. On first glance we may perceive that John might be contentious or seem to take sides if he feels pressured or flustered. Two (2) is the natural number of polarization so different perspectives of any situation will always appear together and seem to contradict what's needed at the time of occurrence. At times, John himself may seem to be a walking contradiction. But to John, he feels buffeted between choices that lose some options for peace but gain others in alternate choices. If he acquiesces to what he doesn't feel comfortable with, people might see his as a people pleaser. If he chooses what makes *him* comfortable, others may see his as being selfish or rebellious. Since the two (2) derives from an eleven (11), he has an option to withdraw from choosing what might appear to be contentious by allowing others to make their own decisions and neither aligning with nor opposing them. The eleven (11) of the *I Ching* gives us this option for *peace*. The eleven (11) is considered the first of what are called *master numbers*. Before we look at *master numbers*, let's first take a look at the *tarot*.

# THE TAROT

As the east has the *I Ching*, the west uses the *Tarot*. The *tarot* is a set of seventy-eight (78) cards expressing the ancient wisdom that originally hailed from Egypt. Accepted as the most authentic deck is the *Rider-Waite* version. Currently there are hundreds of varied decks designed by neophytes and practitioners. The *Rider-Waite* and "standard" decks consists of twenty-two (22) major arcana cards which I will use throughout my delineations and four (4) minor suits numbered one (1) through ten (10) including one knight, queen and king for each suit. I will not address the minor suits except to say that the number cards one (1) through ten (10) can represent the single digits colored by each of the suits either from a physical (earth), emotional (water), mental (air) or intuitive (fire) perspective. I will leave it to the reader to investigate them in more depth in order to expand the meanings and influences of each. Here, I will only use the major arcana as they best represent the numerological system.

It is important to note that each major arcana card's meaning is framed in a perspective of how to or how *not* to address a person or a situation. The *upright* card will tell us what we have going *for* the situation and how we can align with and *augment* its effects. The *reversed* card will tell us what we have going *against* the situation and what we must do to *diminish* its effects. Generally, we can say that the *for* energy is where we are aligned with the natural energies and the *against* energy is how we are either unaware of what is going on or that we are actively working against it as a function of a selfish or egotistical perspective.

*1 - The Magician (Upright)* This is the most creative and proficient card in the deck. It exhibits a sense of potency, effectiveness, sexuality and command of all four (4) elements through having unity within ourselves. The person of this quality is what others call a "shaker and a mover." They are independent and stand alone.

*(Inverted)* There is a person or situation that is missing unity and integrity. Disparate parts create chaos. Parts of the person fights against themselves. This may show as combination of impotency, ineffectiveness, illness and/or absence of vitality.

*(Recommendation)* There is no need to look beyond our current situation or person for what is creative and teeming with potential. Blame does not solve or eliminate ineffectiveness. Take it easy. Be at home. We must work from where we are and know that we are plugged into the source. Everything can move with the ease of expertise.

*2 - The High Priestess (Upright)* The person or situation is filled with secrets and potentials. This is what the Chinese refer to as the "uncarved block." It is a wealth of potential in balance and availability. Its content is a mystery. It is how the feminine energy naturally listens and balances itself through polarities.

*(Inverted)* This card may indicate hidden information or harmful secrets which, if battled against, may cause stress and difficulties for the person or the situation.

*(Recommendation)* When we are surrounded by too many choices and potentials it's best to quiet the outside world and listen to that small voice in the center of our heart. Listen. Stop all action. Quiet the chattering mind. Never mind what methods look better or what advantages can be deduced. Ask yourself what *feels* right?

**3 - *The Empress*** *(Upright)* She is a mother figure and she and/or the situation are pregnant with possibilities. The beginnings are difficult but have the necessary support. The potential for expansion is tremendous.

*(Inverted)* There is either no nurturance available or too much. Things may be pushed to an extreme. There is a disconnect from the source leading to an absence of knowing how far to go. Barren fields grow no corn or too much water floods it. Potential illness can be a result of blocked energy or too much energy.

*(Recommended)* Balanced nurturance of a project or creativity is the best course of action to take now. Do it cautiously. Do it with sensitivity. Be in the moment. Our creativity is expressed best with our full focus. We must learn when is too much or too little.


**4 - *The Emperor*** *(Upright)* We are in control of all four elements. We are extremely competent, sensual, grounded and can easily master the human experience. We may be a mentor, father figure or authority.

*(Inverted)* We can represent a corrupted authority or the quality of being out of control. Sensuality is either absent or too important to us. Materialism is overemphasized. There may be illness, physically, emotionally, mentally as a result of too much or too little self-control.

*(Recommended)* We have to become a lone wolf. We must move to the drumbeat of our own experience. We do not follow the status quo. In being such, we pose a threat to the tribe's security by not supporting collusion in creating a social smoke screen that prevents the exposure of their fears and inadequacies. Depending on their self-perception we may be viewed as either

selfish or a shining example. We likely cannot be fooled or constrained by any system. We are not a true believer.


5 - *The Hierophant* *(Upright)* Our exchanges and communication will be conducted in a conventional and/or formal manner. Sometimes called the Pope the Hierophant epitomizes a conventional authority figure. We will likely behave in a way that people expect us to.

*(Inverted)* We are likely to do things in an unconventional or *seemingly* disorderly manner. We may make others feel uncomfortable or even unsafe. We may be seen as avant-garde or eccentric. In the extreme, we may even devolve into chaos.

*(Recommended)* Convention holds us to a pattern. Many of us feel very secure in that pattern knowing exactly what is expected. When we follow *no* pattern there can be unlimited possibilities. When we follow a pattern, our potential can be curtailed by its structure. We must choose which path to follow depending on the type of energy that is needed or favored.


6 - *The Lovers* *(Upright)* There may be an important decision pending concerning the people or issues. The importance of our values behind our decisions cannot be overemphasized. Choice puts us on a path of commitment. Through our choice we may also create allies or enemies.

*(Inverted)* We may have either made an important decision or we may be procrastinating committing ourselves knowing that we may lose one of our options through committing to one of them. Whether our choice of acting or not is appropriate or not remains to be seen.

*(Recommended)* Before choosing or committing ourselves to a course of action we must ask ourselves is choosing really necessary? Choosing an option for growth is very different from choosing sides in a dispute. We must determine which

choices we are confronted with. If our choice is made through our possessive animal nature it will cause conflict with the passage of time. If our decision is made with a larger scope in mind, our choice may not matter.

**7 - *The Chariot*** *(Upright)* We feel we have command over our animal nature. We have full detachment. Our sensitivities are at peak potential. We feel we have a sense of command and mastery over ourselves and our environment. This may also indicate a trip by road or rail or the initiation or purchase of a "new" vehicle.

*(Inverted)* We feel that he have little or no control over ourselves, our environment or our issues. Our sensitivities are overwhelming us. We are unable to create distance from the influences. Our "vehicle" is in need of repair. A trip is either completed or terminated.

*(Recommended)* When we use our mind or "think" about our issues we can easily become overwhelmed by the polarities within its components. When we are in command of a situation, we have become a witness to our own action or somehow detached from it. Hence, we can sense it more clearly and perform more effective actions in response.

**8 - *Strength*** *(Upright)* This indicates that our animal nature has been integrated with our activities. We feel power in this unity. We have the courage and the stamina but we also have the wider view of things and an understanding of the path our actions, and those of others, will take.

*(Inverted)* We literally, have no strength, no power and no understanding of what forces are governing our issues. We are either afraid to act or are reckless in our approach to things.

*(Recommended)* Having the strength to meet the unknown is a tremendous challenge for all of us. We must have faith; not that

our dreams will be realized as we expect them but that we will have the capacity to recognize the patterns they follow and act on them when they present the opportunity.

**9 - *The Hermit*** *(Upright)* Healing is a valuable commodity. We are either getting and education or giving one. We've learned a lesson. We can also provide insight to others.
*(Inverted)* We have not learned our lesson and/or we are at risk for repeating it. There are many left over issues to tend to. We feel we must be everything to everyone while we can't even take care of ourselves.
*(Recommended)* If we follow our heart and trust in our own experience, we will have what we need to be a beacon for others to emulate and learn from. Show others what we know. If it falls on deaf ears, walk away. Simply do what we need to do in the way we think is proper and we will provide a good example to others.

**10 – *The Wheel of Fortune*** *(Upright)* Issues have come full circle. We can either change our focus or continue on with a completed cycle behind us. Its completion was patterned from the beginning. The "rightness" of its fit may make us feel the outcome was "inevitable."
*(Inverted)* The change or opportunity has occurred. Either we have made a change or missed an opportunity.
*(Recommendation)* We have an opportunity to see the completed cycle and all its contents and polarities before us. Do we see the pattern? Is it what we want? We must choose whether to continue on or change gears.

**11 – *Justice*** *(Upright)* We will handle or are being handled in a fair manner concerning the issues of our attention. Things are aligned, balanced and operating smoothly. All is as it should be.

*(Inverted)* We believe that things are being handled unfairly. We don't see the inequity of our own actions. We believe things should be handled more in our favor.

*(Recommended)* Things are as they are. The reason doesn't matter. We must, resolutely, move through this transition with balance and awareness. We must move past the patterns that have held us in check to continue growing. We must allow old useless patterns to fall away and not panic. Do this with mindfulness.

**12 – The Hanged Man** *(Upright)* We can see things clearly but are unwilling or unable to change them. We see things objectively but they are immovable at the moment.

*(Inverted)* Whatever objectivity is available is insufficient to give complete information. We must trust our gut and fly by the seat of our pants. We see things subjectively. It's easy to move but difficult to know where our actions will end up.

*(Recommended)* As we see both sides of any situation, we realize that taking opposing positions will only serve to exacerbate the polarizing effect as a result. We realize that light and dark must co-exist for balance. Allowing both sides to integrate within us is the best choice. We also know that when we act, we don't see clearly and when we are not acting, we are able to observe the complete picture. Immersion precludes objectivity.

**13 – Death** *(Upright)* Everything has a life span. Whether it's physical, emotional, mental or spiritual; in every death there is potential for birth as illustrated by the white rose. Resistance is futile. We will return to the earth.

*(Inverted)* Transformation has already occurred. However, our refusal to let go of holding on to what we feel that we want or

need for security only increases the stress we face with the people we believe are preventing or blocking our attainment of it. Acceptance by us seem unconscionable.

*(Recommendation)* Growth cannot be taught; only experienced. We can grow willingly or we can go kicking, screaming and fighting. The point is, either way, we *will* grow. The choice is a no-brainer. Aging with grace only comes from the acceptance of the world as we find it. We change what we can, accept what we cannot and recognize the difference.

**14 - *Temperance*** *(Upright)* Issues appear to be in balance. This can relate to health, metabolism, nourishment or any other set of contributing factors that require a rapport between them. Our perspective is such that we feel and recognize that the issues that currently face us are in a delicate balance because we are in balance within ourselves.

*(Inverted)* Issues are out of balance. We are troubled and in need of a perspective that will produce or even allow a feeling of balance within us. This struggle is a very strong contributor to ill health; whether physical, emotional or mental.

*(Recommendation)* Light needs dark to define itself. The reverse is true, also. To favor or deny one emboldens the power of the other through reflection. In this it will seek to resolve itself into balance. The natural tendency toward balance is a most important understanding in alchemy. Balance requires no action. Imbalance requires adjustment: not too much and not too little.

**15 – *The Devil*** *(Upright)* Any form of habit, bondage, conditioning or patterning can be self-perpetuating. These are chosen. These include commitments, contracts, obligations and any form of chronic condition. Commitments have limits.

Contracts have conclusions. To recognize this implies awareness.

(*Inverted*) A commitment or obligation may be finished, terminated or released. In its completion there is freedom from bondage. After initially committing they may also be ignored or avoided. Misuse or coercion of commitments and obligations create manipulation, blackmail, extortion, dependency (emotional or substance), and the bondage of ourselves and others.

(*Recommendation*) What have we been trained into believing about ourselves? How have we been labeled by others? Our public identity doesn't come so much from what we've done but how people choose to see us. If we live within *their* boundaries and assumptions, we may remain included and safe in collusion. Individuals are dangerous. They don't support the illusions used for creating group security. They think for themselves. Notice the chains on the card? They are loose. They can be taken off at any time. We *choose* our bondage through siding with the clan and ignoring what they are too fearful to see. We must do our own thinking. Additionally, choices and commitments must not be conducted in an extreme. These produce enmity and their extreme can be considered fanaticism.

**16 – *The Tower* (Upright)** The pressure between what we personally want or need and what natural law sets in motion is building. The further we resist, the more intense the pressure becomes. This is a test of our sensitivity. It's as if a dam is filling up with water. We have mounting opportunities to become aware and to release the pressure by changing our course. If we do, disaster will be averted. If not, there will be total destruction of our deluded perception of our security.

*(Inverted)* Our resistance could no longer contain the pressure and the issue has exploded.

The worst is over but at tremendous loss…But, like a forest fire, the space has been cleared for new growth. We must now assess the damage and do a cleanup.

*(Recommendation)* We perceive the world through our understanding of how we think it should be. We build our world brick by brick. But when the direction of life changes its course and we don't, the walls begin to sustain a growing pressure. Eventually, the never ceasing change grows past the wall's ability to withstand the external pressure and collapses. Often, the unawareness of our own resistance leads us to be surprised when it does. Unless we learn to recognize a change of course before the pressure goes too far, we will repeat this painful obstinacy again and again. Nothing lasts forever. Least of all, what we insignificant humans put in place to preserve our recognition.


**17 – *The Star*** *(Upright)* A long distance goal gives us the best frame to align our abilities and assets with. With it we feel our life has purpose and direction. With it our challenges become clear. Our intensified focus offers us the opportunity to apply confidence and strength. Will we accept the distance and effort we must traverse to attain it?

*(Inverted)* We don't know where we are going or what we are doing. We feel lost and helpless. We feel discouraged that we see no clear way to get "from here to there." We feel hopeless and paralyzed by our inability to see alternate choices.

*(Recommendation)* Long distance goals are hardest to see when we're preoccupied with resisting an influence. Our best path is often seen after the battle and in the calm after the storm. What we might have resisted so vehemently has passed but what is left is in shambles. Everything has been broken down to its

basic elements. There is no structure to hold on to. We can see for miles with no obstructions. All we can hear is our own heartbeat. Resonate to its rhythm. *This* is the new path.

**18 – *The Moon*** *(Upright)* Our intuitive faculties are registering the world around us at top efficiency and razor sharp. Depending on how vulnerable we feel, this may either be extremely gratifying or terrifying. Empathy can be blessing or a curse. Being in natural balance with the universe is not always the most secure feeling, especially, when there are parts of life we wish to avoid. If we are good with natural balance, we will feel supreme comfort. If not, we will be highly distressed.

*(Inverted)* We feel "out of sync" with "normalcy." Our emotions are running ungoverned. Our ambitions, jealousies and fears are in high gear. Our intuition is in overdrive. We feel like an emotional basket case. The empathy we feel from the world is creating havoc with our emotional balance. We are in dire need of grounding ourselves.

*(Recommendation)* We know we know more that we're able to describe. Yet, are we comfortable enough to allow that to happen? Now, we are prophetic. At our deepest levels, we know the outcome of all we see even before its completion. But is that something to be welcomed or dreaded? Are we ok being someone else's anchor? Do we feel responsible for being so? Remember though, we can lead a horse to water but we can't make them drink. We must drop our seeds and move on. Those who can recognize what we have to offer will find their way. Those who can't must and will find another path and we should feel no guilt if they do.

**19 – *The Sun*** *(Upright)* It seems like we've "come home." There has been or will be a reunion, marriage or rebirth physically, emotionally, mentally or spiritually. There is a feeling of having arrived. It seems like everything has fallen in place.

*(Inverted)* There is a feeling of separation or divorce. The place we're in feels foreign. We feel like we've lost something but don't know what it is, where it is or what or where to look for it.

*(Recommendation)* When our conduct is such that we deal with each situation without preconceptions and as if it is a brand-new set of circumstances, we feel powerful, free and "connected." We find a new experience in everything we do.

**20 – *Judgement*** *(Upright)* When we have expended tremendous effort and feel a judgment of minimal returns, we need to look at the overall pattern that we are passing through. All life progresses through patterns much like seasons. They follow the natural laws of the universe. By contemplating these stages and recognizing what came before our current situation, we can understand where we are and what will come next. Human and worldly events essentially follow the same seasons and patterns. By finding similar beginning stages in other situations, we can begin to see the overall patterns as a reflection of our current situation. We can then see what we need to do to regain our path.

*(Inverted)* Tremendous effort has been applied with no returns. But we have been unable to see the situation from a larger perspective. We are unable to focus on what came before so seeing what's next is out of the question. We can't see the forest from the trees. We feel stuck. Failure.

*(Recommendation)* If we only believe in what we are told we will remain within the cover of a cocoon. There is no room for questioning. Those who don't want to question want to remain in a state of assumed security; aka: illusion. We are afraid to see what might force us to adapt beyond the boundaries of our

familiar and comfortable old patterns. Questioning only occurs in those who are willing to know that there is more than meets the eye and are willing to risk. This leads to the death of some illusions. New experiences replace old judgments and limits.

**21 - *The World*** (*Upright*) There is no limit to what can be done now. The "world is our oyster." We have adjusted our perspective and are able to move past our limits.

(*Inverted*) Things may take a little more time than anticipated. Issues may be postponed or delayed.

(*Recommendation*) No activity ever fully completes itself. It always brings a new door of experience to move through. Opening the door is easy. Closing the one behind us is frightening. We are leaving a world where the puzzle pieces have all fallen into place and *almost* all is known. This provides a tremendous sense of release from the *past*. It's like graduating college. It's the end of "adolescence." After four years of work and accomplishment we must now apply our fruits to a new application. We must now move from being a "big fish in a little pond" to a "little fish in a big pond."

**22 - *The Fool*** (*Upright*) He indicates a brand-new decision or experience. With it comes inexperience as to what is needed to handle the new situation for the new and "innocent." However, if we have prior experience and have been modest enough not to push ourselves on the environment due to any bias or preconceptions, we approach the brand new with eyes of a child and the patience of a master.

(*Inverted*) This new opportunity either has already transpired, been missed or turned down.

(*Recommendation*) Remember that this is a new opportunity for experience. There are no guide posts as to behaviors or choices. It is necessary to approach this new situation without any preconceptions or judgments. Others may think us crazy for this attitude. Fostering innocence, being in the moment and trusting our inner feeling is the best path to follow.

## TAROT SUMMARY

Although the cards themselves don't relate directly to the numerological values, their individual meanings do incorporate much of what the symbolism speaks of. The meaning will generally convey the broader beaning of the number as applied to overall circumstances occurring in the life of our client. Other factors such as the *birth path*, *personal years* and the three (3) name vibrations carried and hopefully utilized. Closer examination of the matrix of influences must be used as to determine the actual applications of any of the major arcana cards. Please use careful judgment in order to  avoid jumping to conclusions about their meaning or importance.

# MASTER NUMBERS

Numbers that are the same double digits are regarded as *master numbers*. These are eleven (11), twenty-two (22), thirty-three (33), forty-four (44), fifty-five (55), sixty-six (66), seventy-seven (77), eighty-eight (88) and ninety-nine (99). On first glance one would assume that they simply double the effect of the primary number. But *master numbers* offer much more than a simple augmentation of effect and the depth of understanding required to comprehend their meaning, let alone our ability to wield them, is well beyond the average person.

*Master numbers* only present an opportunity for performing with excellence and emotional maturity above and beyond individual endeavors. Almost everyone have *master numbers* that their single digit vibrations draw from. They may be obvious or hidden. However, their effect is not dependent on their visibility. They require an expanded consciousness and awareness in order to be activated. There are many people who claim "mastery" of *master numbers* while their actions remain centered only on their own personal benefit. To activate *master numbers* our intention and actions must go beyond any need for personal recognition or accomplishment. The biggest difference in the potential use of *master numbers* is whether our life perspective is directed toward egotistical avenues or emotionally mature pursuits. As we look at each of the *master numbers*, we can gain an understanding of what is needed in focus and performance.

In discussing any *master number*, we must first begin with understanding its relationship to the single digit it reduces to. Eleven (11) reduces to a two (2). The most dominant vibration of a two (2) is polarization or the tendency for it to separate any focus or situation into opposing influences. Let's look first at the egotistical side of eleven over two (11/2).

When we are challenged in our life pursuits and our self-image does not allow us the perception of being on an equal footing with our peers, our family and the general public, we perceive the world as a competition for survival and dominance over the advantage we have, or not, over others. This perspective represents the *majority* of our population. Always remember that we are all still part animal, even if our religions or cultural identities tell us differently. The urge to survive and dominate is innately buried in all of us. However, even if we deny our animal origins, this feeling always exists just below the surface of our conscious focus. The two (2) vibration is a stark representative of our human competition and survival-oriented mind-set, especially, since its method is to create separation, polarization and advantage. Nature has no such "attitude" in its structure in that it constantly moves toward rebalancing inequities, dulling sharp edges and smoothing out the differences between night and day. It is the human psyche that is born into a perceived separation from nature and the balance that it constantly provides. As we grow within our family, our separation from the world is emphasized through family clan "specialization" of character and values. These are the qualities that identify us as traditionally separate from the whole. Within each traditional clan we are further separated out into being acceptable by them or not. With this type of mind-set, it's only natural that what we will do will be designed with the intention of advancing our self-image in our family, our clan and the world. Depending on which level of unity is desired, our family, clan or social group, will tell us to what degree we will compromise personal advantage for how selfish we will be. Our egotistical boundaries are determined by how much we need our personal advantage to be felt or acknowledged by others.

The more we are willing or able to compromise our personal needs, desires and requirements is an indicator of our emotional maturity. That is, the wider is our focus and acceptance of humanity as it is, the more emotionally mature we are and the more we will have aligned with nature's movement toward rebalancing inequities, dulling sharp edges and smoothing out the differences between night and day. Hence, the more we live in separation, the more animal we are. The more we allow the universe to express itself in the diverse world as it is and *without* our need to prevail and make ourselves dominant in it, the more we live in unity, and the closer we come to aligning with our spirit. In the *Tao Te Ching* Lao Tzu said "The Way is gained through daily loss."

Our egotistical side is expressed in the polarized two (2). Our unity with spirit is expressed through the eleven (11). The eleven (11) is two unities coexisting with each other, one (1) and one (1), without interfering with each other. Hence, the *I Ching* relates eleven (11) as *peace* or prospering.

When a person activates the eleven (11) in their potential, they do or allow what's best for *both themselves and for others*. They find a way that everyone involved benefits from whatever is being dealt with. It is composed of a wide minded view of self as being part of the whole. Choice is not for or against but with. He or she allows the polarization by others but acts to achieve the natural balance between the two. Sometimes it brings them personal gain. Sometimes it brings them personal loss. But it always brings balance between polarized factions. Working in this way the person may be viewed by polarized people as selfish, cowardly, neglectful, abusive or any number of qualities used to define an egotistical person's identity as "special" as a compensation for their damaged self-image.

To activate or even recognize the proper use of the eleven (11), a person must eliminate a damaged self-image through forgiveness of self, forgiveness of others and have the awareness and a willingness to work *for the benefit of the world with their inclusion in the manifesting of the whole.*

## MASTER NUMBER 22

Twenty-Two (22) reduces to a four (4). The most dominant vibration of a four (4) is tangibility, sensuality and materialism or a tendency to relate everything to the physical and tangible world. Let's look first at the egotistical side of twenty-two over four (22/4).

"I'm from Missouri, show me" is usually a statement that you might hear when someone has a dominant four (4). There is a tendency for people with a strong influence of four (4) to bring everything back to a tangible or factually justifiable reference.

Generally, they feel out of control emotionally, and it leads them to trust and invest only in things that have tangible boundaries. Boundaries provide the physical evidence that the four (4) tends to bring forward. Physical structure is the primary domain of the four (4). Hence, work, building and disassembling are its primary agents. When something is physical, its borders can be defined in a way that a person with a dominant four (4) can feel secure and exacting. This allows them to feel in control.

People born with a strong four (4) often don't feel comfortable or in control of themselves when dealing with feelings or emotions. These qualities have no boundaries or edges that can be clearly defined by their senses. Hence, they have no clear understanding of who or where they are. This leads them to feel that the only place they can feel in control of their life is in that which is tangible or felt by their senses or rationalized by their mind. If they grow up in a family where feelings and emotions are the primary tool of relating, it will push them into becoming more physically oriented allowing them to feel more in control, especially, if those feelings or emotions are used to control or dominate them. For them, this also diminishes the value of feelings and emotions and heightens their trust in the mental and physical. In this case the mental may appear as intangible but remembering that the mind uses separation as its discrimination, it can have exacting boundaries which works well with the senses.

Often, children with heavy four (4) components are brought up in environments where feelings and emotions are used as validations for who and what they are required to be, do and be responsible for. One or more of the parents may base their perception of the world on what they feel rather than what they actually do or think. Since the four (4) feels out of their depth when feelings and emotions are used, they will lean much more into basing their world validation on their senses. When a child is brought up being deceived or manipulated out of their autonomy through emotional means, they tend to lean harder into trusting only what their senses can validate for them. For them emotions and feelings of others then become unimportant.

As heavy four (4) vibration children get older, more "mature" and grounded in accepting only tangible evidence for what is true, problems evolve when they start expecting everyone else to validate *themselves* only by what *they* physically sense or think. Expecting others to accept and receive them on only their terms will appear arrogant and presumptuous. Others then will become unsympathetic of them as they will assume that the four (4) person is uncaring and lacking humility or compassion. The person operating by a four (4) vibration will see these people as unsupportive, irresponsible, and undependable. They will feel like they must do everything themselves. They will feel as if all they do is work, work and work. They will then feel entitled to act without consideration for others and only work for and do what benefits themselves. This will tend to make others think that the four (4) person is opportunistic and will ignore if not avoid them. Why others won't be supportive them will remain a mystery to them.

The twenty-two (22) vibration works on a whole different level of maturity. In the *I Ching* it is referred to as *grace*. As a twenty-two over four (22/4) progresses in age, maturity and life experience, they often find that they are much more successful in their endeavors if the projects that they are involved in are more group oriented than personally directed. After in-depth soul searching and personal experience, they have come to recognize the futility of attempting to maintain personal control over others for their own security and personal satisfaction.

When success occurs in a group, the results are often multiplied logarithmically. Everyone seems to benefit more from group success than personal success. Group members also return support to the mature twenty-two over four (22/4) worker because they know that what they do benefits not only themselves but that they enable an inclusiveness that benefits everyone. Virtually no one is left out. They are not sacrificed either. Being wide minded and doing what benefits every member of the group, including themselves, encourages the group's trust, honor, respect and support for the twenty-two over four (22/4) worker. If that worker has also been blessed with having chosen to exhibit humility and compassion, their respect and personal rewards reach even further. The personal sacrifice that the twenty-two over four (22/4) worker exhibits comes from the understanding that to *compromise*, not give up, personal benefit synchronizes with the larger whole and gains the universe's support free of the separateness and competition that are so typical of the person operating on a simple four (4) mentality and perspective. The small-minded selfishness that feeds only personal pleasure, satisfaction and security is absent in the true twenty-two over four (22/4).

Having a twenty-two over four (22/4) in our makeup *only provides an opportunity for success*. There are no guarantees that anything striven for will be successful, especially, if the execution of the efforts are primarily directed at personal security or advantage over others.

<hr>

## MASTER NUMBER 33

<hr>

Thirty-Three (33) reduces to a six (6). Six (6) is the number of choices, decisions, priorities and commitment. If these qualities can refer to the values and commitments that are best for the larger whole, the potential for the thirty-three (33) can be realized. If these values and commitments are only viewed from only an individual's preferences, beliefs and needs for security, the lower vibration of the six (6) is likely to take precedence. The *I Ching* holds the number thirty-three (33) as *retreat* or *yielding*. It holds the number six (6) as *conflict*. There is a world of difference between the two. Let's take a look at the dynamics of the six (6) first.

Six (6) is the number that deals with our values. We, or those who train us, decide what is important to us. If we grow toward into being balanced, mature and strong, we decide ourselves and do not force our choices on those around us. If we do not, we yield to whatever the group we wish to belong to says is important or we rebel against it. The essence of this weakness is what brings inner *conflict*.

There are three way we can deal with this *conflict*: we can honestly yield, we can honestly rebel or we can outwardly yield and inwardly rebel through passive aggression. However, all three approaches derive from a deficit in our self-image. Our self-image may have minor discrepancies or major friction. The intensity of our compliance, rebellion or passive aggressiveness will be proportional to degree of discord within our self-image.

The stronger the discord, the stronger the response. The milder the discord, the more benign the response.

Now ask yourself, what do you really feel passionate about? Why? How much can you allow others to be or do what contradicts your values? The quicker you react, the more intense the *conflict*. Now ask yourself how much you were allowed to follow your own beliefs and values as child? Were you pushed or forced into adopting values that go against your core feelings? Is your passion a reflection of your upbringing? Is there a *conflict* or is there a strong alignment with your mentors? Parents who demanded a strong commitment or parents who supported your choice of commitment have set the stage for how you handle the values and commitments *chosen by others*. The more strongly your values were coerced or encroached on, the stronger your trigger for participating in *conflict* will be. The more you were allowed to assert your own choice, the less likely you will be to be triggered by someone else's opposing claims.

Thirty-three (33) in the *I Ching* speaks of *retreat*, withdrawal or yielding. On hearing the word *retreat* we might first think of wars and battles. But in any situation that embraces *conflict*, war might be the extreme or simple disagreement might be the case. How capable we are of handling *conflict*, or not, is largely a function of our upbringing. If we were allowed and trusted to make our own choices, the potential for our being drawn into *conflict* may be minor. If we were coerced into accepting values other than of our own choosing, the potential for being drawn into *conflict* will be much stronger. Our primary tool for dealing with *conflict* is our ability to detach from the circumstances that create its trigger.

A major contributing factor in someone's inability to "let something go" is something that seems to diminish their pride. However, pride is often a defense against feelings of inadequacy or incompetence. The more inadequate we feel, the more prideful we will tend to be. If we can allow someone to "save face," the intensity toward getting pulled into *conflict* will be diminished and they will no longer feel the need to validate their values. Our retreat from the need to validate our own values usually allows another to back down from defending theirs. Hence, the feeling of inadequacy that generated the need no longer risks exposure. The stronger we are in *our* self-image, the more able we will be able to detach from pride triggering influences. Our image in the minds of others may be diminished. Others may think us a coward or spineless. But, if we *know* this is *not* true, it will be easy for us to yield. If we *believe* this is *true*, it will be much more difficult to detach and let their assumptions of us to stand.

In sacrificing our pride, we diminish our potential for being drawn into *conflict*. If the *conflict* is not life threatening, we should have little or no trouble making a timely *retreat* or withdrawal. The person with an active thirty-three over six (33/6) vibration has untangled themselves from being invested in how others judge and assess them. They have learned to commit to and trust in the values that *they* have decided are true and proper for them. They are no longer triggered by the accusations or insults coming from others that might incite their pride and any fear of inadequacy that it might have covered. Accomplishment and recognition are no longer part of their intended destination. Their values are the only issue of substance. They willingly commit only to those values that benefit the larger whole, even if it might require the ultimate sacrifice. Selflessness is one of their highest qualities as it applies to becoming one with spirit of the White Brotherhood and the Christ consciousness.

---

## MASTER NUMBER 44

---

Forty-four (44) reduces to an eight (8). Eight (8) is representative of organization, cycles, patterns and discipline. Everything in the physical universe operates within these disciplined patterns and cycles. The *I Ching* relates to eight (8) as *unity* or holding together. The *I Ching* relates to forty-four (44) as *temptation* and avoiding evil. This is appropriate because the *temptation* of those with a dominant forty-four over eight (44/8) is to control, use and exploit the world for personal benefit. Forty-four (44) is the number of the world server. This is one of the hardest points in development for a human to maintain emotional balance. Let's first take a look at the eight (8) to see why.

The recognitions of the patterns that life follows is a boon for the awareness of those who have a dominant eight (8) in their makeup. It enables the person who recognizes this to tap into the natural flow of energy and ride the movement to its completion with a minimum of extra effort. Eight (8) is a representative of the law which talks about the conservation of energy. Recognizing this law in action eliminates the tendency that those who are ignorant of it have toward "pushing the river" to the completion of their objectives. This wastes a tremendous amount of energy. Those who become aware of it easily "step into the current" and are aided in moving toward their objectives smoothly and easily. To recognize this and do it for ourselves is rewarding and commendable. But to recognize the flow and efforts of others and step into *their* flow usurping the benefits of *their* work is selfish and opportunistic and keeps us in an exclusively "one way" and personally beneficial mindset. Those who have the forty-four over eight (44/8) potential but act solely toward personal advantage over others cannot activate the broader influence of its potential. Personal focus keeps them polarized and the growth into spiritual maturity is wasted. This comes from polarizing of the work applied by the two fours (4) against each other.

A selfish perspective in the eight (8) vibration can be used to divide, distract and create opposition in the two contributing fours (4). The personalized and perverted influence of the forty-four over eight (44/8) is the tool of a tyrant. *Aligning* the efforts of each of the fours (4) toward a universally beneficial objective is the mark of an actualized forty-four over eight (44/8) vibration and a world server such as Gandhi and Kennedy. The size of the effect can be clan oriented or on the world stage. The effects can be felt in small venue as well as on a world venue: as above, so below.

## MORE MASTER NUMBERS

The master numbers I have covered thus far are the more conventionally known and used numbers. But master numbers don't stop there. The pattern of double digits continues but in a significantly different realm. Let me explain.

Master numbers eleven (11), twenty-two (22), thirty-three (33) and forty-four (44) all reduce to *even* single digits. (2,4,6 & 8). *Even* numbers are the building blocks of the physical world because they all support the physical world tendency toward *polarization*. All the dynamics powering the physical world are based on their *polarity* in order to be recognized. If we notice black, it is because we also know white. If we notice the ability to have, we know this because in our time on this earth we have felt lack. If we recognize up, it is because we also know down. Everything in the physical world is built on the concept of opposites. Separation, or the existence of opposites, is the quality of life that enables our awareness. That is, we become aware of something because it is different from what we know or wasn't there before. The reason we don't notice the effects of the continuing *odd* master numbers is that they do not produce the same tangible physical results like the first four sets that reduce to *even* and *polarizing* numbers. Those of us who are less aware only notice what happens in the materialistically polarized world. Inner influences that reduce to *odd* numbers primarily affect us *internally* and often go unrecognized.

The continuing master numbers are fifty-five (55), sixty-six (66), seventy-seven (77), eighty-eight (88) and ninety-nine (99). You will notice that they all reduce to first, an *even* two-digit number, and then to a single digit *odd* number. (55-10-1, 66-12-3, 77-14-5, 88-16-7, & 99-18-9). That two-digit *even* number is how they will appear to the physical world. The single digit *odd* number is how they will affect us internally. Let's now take a look at each set.

---

## MASTER NUMBER 55

---

Fifty-five (55) reduces first to a ten (10) and then to a one (1). The *I Ching* calls fifty-five (55) the *zenith* or a pinnacle. This is the highest arrival point where everything we have done has brought us to. For a moment, the changes of one polarity (5) are now in balance with the changes of the opposing polarity (5).

When we throw a ball up in the air, there is a point where it rests before it changes direction. This is the peak point in its travel before it begins its decline to its point of origin. When the Moon goes through her phases, she becomes full as her *zenith* and then begins her decline toward the beginning of a new cycle. Everything in the world moves in cycles. Every cycle has a *zenith*. Every cycle begins a decline after arriving at its *zenith*. It is human nature to attempt to hold ourselves at our full Moon. That part of us is the animal part which attempts to keep our current tangible accomplishment present in the physical world. But as we all know, life moves on. Things change. The world continues with or without our participation. We cannot hold on to the outside world full Moon. Life forces us to let go and move on.

Although the physical *zenith* may pass, the feeling of it remains within us. Our arrival at it was accomplished through a process. This process consists of patterns of *conduct* that enabled us to arrive at that balance point. Renewing this *conduct* enables us to recreate the *feeling* within us. We know this *conduct* to be the result of having performed with the "right behavior" and lining us up with our past *zenith* of accomplishment. Hence, acting in the same way produces the same feeling enabling the *zenith* to shine and live on *within us*.

The ten (10) that the fifty-five (55) reduces to is said to be *conduct* or "right behavior" in the *I Ching*. It reminds us that if there is a place or goal that we wish to see ourselves at or in, we must follow the energy pattern that animates that goal. As we align with its energy pattern, we create the potential for its manifestation. Even though the physical goal may have passed its peak, following the energy pattern can recreate the feeling within us. Is there anything more that we really need? If we feel that we need the physical manifestation, aren't we are looking for approval or justification from the world? External proof isn't necessary for those of us who believe in ourselves. For those of us who are emotionally balanced, the feeling will be enough.

The ten (10) now reduces to a one (1). The *I Ching* calls the one (1) *the creative*. For anything to come into manifestation there needs to be an alignment of its components. This is the *unity* we spoke of when we delineated the one (1). Align with the energy pattern of "right behavior" and the potential for manifestation presents itself. But that manifestation, like all *odd* numbers, is internal.

All that is done with the fifty-five over ten over one (55/10/1) may begin in the external world through our responses to it but must eventually coalesce to an internal use and understanding of the vibration. All the qualities listed in the one (1) *birth path* will also apply.

---

### MASTER NUMBER 66

---

Sixty-six (66) reduces first to a twelve (12) and then to a three (3). The sixty-six (66) is the first of our master numbers who does not have a compliment in the *I Ching*. Because master numbers are *even* and have a representation in the physical world, must look at the *pair* of balanced sixes (6). We know six (6) to represent choice, values, priorities and commitment. But we must also remember that six (6) brings *conflict* through its *choice*, especially, because when paired with another six (6), the *choices* or commitments will be opposed or balanced against another *choice* or commitment of equal value and intensity. As long as the values remain balanced and at equal intensity, *conflict* remains at a standstill. When one set of values under the six (6) begins to take precedence or dominance over the other, then the *conflict* is activated. When they are in that momentary balance or standstill, *stagnation* or an impasse of the twelve (12) occurs as per the *I Ching*. Also, the tarot major arcana number twelve (12), *The Hanged Man* is brought in as an influence. Depending on our perspective, we either *see* the situation clearly and are *unable* or *unwilling* to change it or we *don't* see it clearly and we *are* able and willing to take action. This impasse or *stagnation* is observable in the physical world because it is still a polarized and *even* number. In that *stagnation*, impasse, and momentary standstill, the three (3) is born of the twelve (12).

The three (3) is a struggle towards birth and is called *difficult beginnings* in the *I Ching*. Remember too that the Empress, the pregnant goddess, is key number three (3) in the tarot major arcana. The fertilized egg begins to develop into a male or female, aka, one set of values or *choices* begins to take dominance over the other. As with the yin and yang, balance (unfertilized) inevitably yields to change (fertilized) and a third entity begins to form. That entity could be a child, an idea, a project, a belief or any other polarize entity. Like a seed, the growth and expansion of the *odd* number three (3) first happens *internally* under the earth, within the womb before it bursts upon the tangible earth. All the qualities and struggle of the *birth path* three (3) begin to showing rapid growth and expansion with little or no apparent regulation as to its speed.

---

## MASTER NUMBER 77

Seventy-seven (77) reduces first to a fourteen (14) and then to a five (5). With no *I Ching* representation, seventy-seven (77) will probably be the *least* recognized vibration in the tangible world as the seven (7) is composed of subtleties. The balance will be felt only by those with enough sensitivity to discriminate between two changing and interlocking empathies. These will be the smoothly moving undercurrents. Much like if we dropped oil in moving water, the two would not blend or dissolve but swirl around each other's texture and penetrate each other's depth. Here there would be no struggle due to the polarities but a definite sensing of each liquid's boundaries.

In this, the "acceptance" of each other's presence, there would appear the *sovereignty,* quiet "integrity" and power of the seventy-seven's (77) reduction to the number fourteen (14) in the *I Ching*. Key fourteen (14) of the tarot *major arcana, Temperance,* would also be apparent in the patience and balance perceived between the two forces. This quiet power and integrity would be analogous to the meeting of two highly influential leaders. Both have power and force but not visible to the non-sensitive observers. Yet, under the respectful regard and formalities exhibited between each leader, the interplay of the undercurrents between them are establishing the boundaries and limits for any negotiations that would ensue. As all their boundaries are discovered and acknowledged, the *sovereignty* of the fourteen (14) would reduce down through the *I Ching's patience* of the five (5) and *change* and *exchange* would ensue. Both leaders would, in a sense, evolve *internally* and the change in each of their *inner* perspectives would soon become communicated to the world. The public would be unaware of what took place in the negotiations themselves and would only become aware of any change by what was ultimately communicated to them. In the leaders, there still may be undercurrents as yet unresolved.

## MASTER NUMBER 88

Eighty-eight (88) reduces first to a sixteen (16) and then to a seven (7). Eighty-eight (88) is a pair of eights (8) that holds each of the polarized and organized structures in check against each other. This is sort of like checks and balances in government when it actually works as planned. This is also like two or more businesses where the prices are kept at a specific level because they are actually in competition with each other. Of course, each could also collude to fix prices but, either way, a balance will be maintained. Each of their moves and changes provokes a response on the part of the others. Again, we're dealing with *polarization* that could obviously be recognized in government and business but is also present in relationships but on less of a perceivable scale.

When all works well, the energies may continue to remain in balance if handled maturely over time. But we're all human and eventually opportunism creeps in, especially in relationships while being conscious or not, and small changes in each escalates the pressure between the two eights (8). If both persons are mature and are willing to allow compromise in the relationship, all will continue to work well. The sixteen (16) that the eighty-eight (88) reduces to will then show the *adapting* that the *I Ching* speaks about. But if lack of awareness or immaturity become the case, *The Tower* in the tarot *major arcana* will build an intensity between them that will reach a point beyond each participant's ability to maintain control. In other words, one or both eights (8) build up a tremendously conflicting pressures aimed at gaining personal advantage over the other which is resisted or countered by the other eight (8). An explosion ultimately results returning the pressure to manageable levels. This is the reason that in many older numerology books eighty-eight over seven (88/7) has been regarded as a signet of disaster.

The seven (7) that the eighty-eight (88) and sixteen (16) reduces from is represented in the *I Ching* as *the army*. Since the seven (7) can be viewed from either a sensitive or insensitive perspective, it can represent the gathering of either a compromising energy pathway or an antagonistic energy reservoir. The compromising energies resulting from mature perspectives in a relationship can lead to the dissipation of conflicting energies and the antagonistic reservoir can result in following an immature pathway leading toward the increase of tensions and pressures. Again, due to the odd number quality of the seven (7), these buildups or releases will be mostly internal and not perceivable by the world until an explosion occurs.

---

## MASTER NUMBER 99

Ninety-nine (99) reduces first to an eighteen (18) and then to a nine (9). With no correspondence for the ninety-nine (99) in the *I-Ching* or the tarot, we simply have a pair of nines (9) in balance with each other. With the average person nine (9) symbolizes the need for cleaning up loose ends and leftovers of issues that we might be unaware of or even avoidant of. These are things that will most certainly get in the way of any new endeavors requiring a "clean slate." Nine (9) also lends energy to the feeling that we must *be* all things to all people and at the same time. When we have one set of issues that needs to be considered for only one person, it's a relatively easy fix by prioritizing what needs to be done and following through on our list. But what if we have more than one person with cleanup issues that get in the way of or even causes conflict between each other in what needs to be done overall? This will make us feel helpless and caught between "a rock and a hard place." When this occurs, the situation can deteriorate very rapidly. The ninety-nine (99) then reduces to an eighteen (18).

The *I Ching* relates to eighteen (18) as *decay*. We could then say that any semblance of order seeming to fall apart is in need of repair. However, we must also realize that all situations change, and this may simply be happening within the natural order of things exemplifying going through birth, life and finally death. The tarot *major arcana* key eighteen (18) is *The Moon*. The energy behind the upright card or positive key represents the emotional balance of our feelings and emotions. This gels very nicely with groups of people whose "loose ends" are essentially in alignment with each other. The energy behind the inverted card or negative key embodies feeling and emotions that are out of balance and discordant. This corresponds to relationships, people and groups whose feelings and emotions are discordant and out of whack with each other. Eighteen (18) eventually reduces back to a single nine (9).

A single nine (9) is the distilled result of contending with conflicting loose ends, extracting unnecessary factors and prioritizing the remaining elements. This will most always be done internally. It may become visible to the public but only if disseminated by the individual doing the distilling. This process will also refine and streamline the applicable factors that may be retained and invested by the individual into new projects as they go through the distilling process.

# PUTTING IT ALL TOGETHER

So far, we have been dealing with everything piecemeal. We know that the *birth path* gives us the direction, *personal years* give us timing and our names, given or chosen, give us the qualities that we can or must work with and through. But when we all put these factors together, we can observe a roadmap of *when* we have the opportunity to work with each of those qualities in order to refine and integrate them. The *personal years* give us the sequence of the issues that will be dealt with.

| Age | Year | Yr# |
|---|---|---|
| 75 | 2024 | 1 |
| 74 | 2023 | 9 |
| 73 | 2022 | 8 |
| 72 | 2021 | 7 |
| 71 | 2020 | 6 |
| 70 | 2019 | 5 |
| 69 | 2018 | 4 |
| 68 | 2017 | 3 |
| 66 | 2016 | 2 |
| 65 | 2015 | 1 |

|  | 6 | 16 / 7 | 9 | = 31 / 4 |
|---|---|---|---|---|
|  | John | George | Smith |  |
|  | 14 / 5 | 23 / 5 | 15 / 6 | = 52 / 7 |
|  | 20 / 2 | 39 / 12 / 3 | 24 / 6 | = 83 / 11 / 2 |

On the chart on the left we have a ten-year span of *personal years* for John George Smith. This will show us the sequence of potential changes available to him throughout those years. However, if we also include the name in our deliberations, we can assess what kinds of issues will be dealt with, in what years and in what areas of his life. In the chart on the right, we have the full name with just the totals on the right for the *soul urge, quiet self* and *expression* and the vibrations above and below for each name. The bottom line represents the *expressions* and the top and middle lines represent the *soul urge* and the *quiet self* for each name respectively. We now have all the data we need to determine what issues John will be dealing with and when.

With our current year at 2021, we know that John is in a *personal year* of seven (7). If we look at his name, we see that seven (7) resonates with his emotional *soul urge* of seven (7) and the *quiet self* for the whole name. Remember that our middle name represents the emotional component of what our names each give us. The seven (7) *soul urge* for the middle name tells us that he will be highly sensitive to what he desires emotionally. The seven (7) also calls for a sense of emotional detachment from chaotic or insensitive people in his life. Whether he is conscious of it or not, this year will accentuate behaviors to that end as performed through his full *quiet self* which resonates with his middle name *soul's urge*. In any relationship he may be aware of his need for emotional space or he may even question his own emotional behavior as being a sort of self sabotage relative towards intimacy in relationships.

If John is involved in anything artistic or create, this will be a great year to express his sensitivity through that work. He may also react badly to anything, artwork or otherwise, that is garish or gross. The seven (7) vibration will likely make him hypersensitive while encouraging him to seek more alone time than he normally would.

As there are no eight (8) vibrations in his name, there will be no emphasis on any of his name qualities or deficits. This will mean that 2022 will be a relatively quiet year in terms of using or developing specific name qualities and abilities. Only the patterns described under the generic eight (8) *personal year* section will apply.

His nine (9) *personal year* in 2023 will bring a few cleanups and conclusions. You will notice that John's family heritage *soul urge* resonates to a nine (9). This says what John feels or believes what his family wants *for* him or *of* him or what *he* wants *for* his family or *of* them is healing, cleanup, service and many other of the qualities represented by a general nine (9) vibrations. His nine (9) *personal year* may bring an awareness of these desires to the forefront of his awareness where he will have the opportunity to address them, adjust his output toward his family and to reassess what they expect of him. If he is not aware, as is often the case with *soul urge* vibrations, he may find himself in a confusing melee of undercurrents coming from his family or the rising change of his feelings toward them as a result of the surfacing of these issues. In the long run and with or without his awareness, nines (9) always seem to resolve themselves in a simplifying or streamlining of issues. "Cleaning out the closets" is inevitable.

If we look back at the preceding years, we can see that 2016 presented him with opportunities to work on his relationships during a two (2) *personal year* which involved his full *expression* with emphasis on physical issues (first name). During this year he met his future wife.

2017 gave him the opportunity to evolve and build the *expression* of his emotional rapport (middle name *expression*) during a three (3) *personal year*.

2018 gave him the opportunity to realize the solidity desired by his full *soul urge* of four (4). This year he married is current wife and moved in with her.

2019 gave him the opportunity to refine his physical abilities during a five (5) year of his first name *quiet self*. During this year he earned a black belt in martial arts.

2020 brought the opportunity to solidify his commitments during a six (6) year as expressed through his last name *quiet self* and *expression*. Family responsibilities presented themselves as he answered the requirements for tending to an elderly relative.

You can bet that all the issues begun in this nine (9) year cycle will have their origins in what was begun in his personal one (1) year in 2015. During this time, he invested in many new endeavors including beginning martial arts training and applying himself into physical health. 2024 will begin a brand new nine (9) year cycle.

## THE EXCURSION CHART

The *excursion chart* is similar to above but offers a sequential picture of how the *personal years* coordinate with the progression of letters in each name. They also offer a transitional view in terms of how each name begins and ends its own individual cycle. That is, our physical, emotional and traditional names each begin and end through a number of years in an individually cyclic fashion. Let's take a look at how the *excursion chart* is set up.

| Age | YR | F | M | L | T | PY |
|---|---|---|---|---|---|---|
| 0 | 49 | J | G | S | 9 | 7 |
| 1 | 50 | O | G | M | 8 | 8 |
| 2 | 51 | O | G | M | 8 | 9 |
| 3 | 52 | O | G | M | 8 | 1 |
| 4 | 53 | O | G | M | 8 | 2 |
| 5 | 54 | O | G | I | 4 | 3 |
| 6 | 55 | O | G | I | 4 | 4 |
| 7 | 56 | H | E | I | 4 | 5 |
| 8 | 57 | H | E | I | 4 | 6 |
| 9 | 58 | H | E | I | 4 | 7 |

At first, we notice that there are seven columns. The first column is John's age, beginning with zero being in the year of his birth which is correspondingly listed in the second column. This will follow through all the way to the end of the chart until age eighty-four (84) which is, astrologically, our life expectancy. You will find a copy of a blank chart to work with in the appendix. You may copy this chart and fill it in appropriately with your own information. I will provide the examples needed to work with John's *excursion* and others as we move on.

Columns three (3), four (4) and five (5) are for John's physical, emotional and traditional names respectively. The data entry is simple. Start with the first letter of the first name which is (J). Because (J) is a one (1) vibration, list (J) once in the first box under the physical name column. The second letter of the first name is (O). (O) is a six (6) vibration. List (O) in the following boxes six (6) times. Follow through with (H) being listed eight (8) times and (N) being listed five (5) times. At nineteen, John finishes the sequence of his first name. This ends his first *physical* cycle. Now begin again. After finishing with the last (N) of his first name, follow in the next box with one (J) by beginning your input again for a new cycle with starting at age twenty (20), with the first name letters. The shorter and smaller the first name and its corresponding numbers, the more often a new first name or physical cycle will begin again within the eighty-four (84) year life span.

When you've finished entering the first name, now begin by entering (G) seven (7) times under the middle name column, or the emotional name, and follow through with the full middle name sequence of letters and begin again when you arrive at the last letter. Do the same for the last name and its letters until the full chart is completed at age eighty-four (84) for the first, middle and last names.

The chart at any point may be addressed for important influences. For example, simply looking at the beginning sample chart above we can see that at birth John's first transiting emotional letter, (G), is a seven (7) which resonates with his *birth path*, which is also a seven (7). This would say that at his birth there were important emotional influences present at and surrounding his birth. These may temper his reactions to the circumstances surrounding him or from and with his immediate family and those close to him. These emotional influences will set the stage for how he deals with feelings and emotions throughout his coming life. We only need to look at the possible influences that a seven (7) might create in order to understand their bearing on his life.

At age seven (7) (oddly enough), he moves into a five (5) year at the same time that his emotional transiting letters change to an (E) which is also a five (5) vibration. We can safely say that there will be some kind of change in his environment and the way that he relates to it that will cause his emotional demeanor to change. This might be the loss of a parent through death or divorce, a move or any other number of circumstances that can change his emotional disposition through an environmental subtraction or addition of people or circumstances. Seeing this, and especially at this age, we must query our client to know what transpired.

On of the occurrences I've noticed in the *excursion chart* is that when the total of the transiting letters matched up with the personal year, life changing circumstances, almost always with physical evidence, occurred for the client. It's as if the energies lined up and the client couldn't help themselves but to react in a reactive fashion. Those who were more in control of their own fate were often proactive in their responses to the aligning energies. For example, in the next example the totals and the transiting letters lined up differently in two years.

| 32 | 81 | H | L | E | 16/7 | 3 |
| 33 | 82 | H | L | E | 16/7 | 4 |
| 34 | 83 | H | A | E | 14/5 | 5 |
| 35 | 84 | N | W | E | 15/6 | 6 |
| 36 | 85 | N | W | E | 15/6 | 7 |
| 37 | 86 | N | W | R | 19/1 | 8 |

In this *excursion chart* segment this client met their spouse to be of twenty years in their thirty-fourth (34) year. Notice that the total letter vibration of fourteen over five (14/5) matches the same five (5) vibration corresponding to a *personal year* of change. You will also note that the total vibration of the thirty-fifth year of 15/6 matches the *personal year* of six (6) during which they got married.

| 38 | 87 | N | W | R | 19/1 | 9 |
| 39 | 88 | N | W | R | 19/1 | 1 |
| 40 | 89 | -J- | R | R | 19/1 | 2 |

In the next example at age thirty-nine (39) we see that the total vibration of the letters of nineteen over one (19/1) align again with a one (1) *personal year*. In this year they moved to a new state and took the business they began with them. The nineteen over one (19/10/1) shows the approach of the nineteen (19), conduct of the ten (10) and the new ventures and independence of the one (1) exemplifying what was required of them to do so.

| 42 | 91 | O | R | R | 24/6 | 4 |
| 43 | 92 | O | R | R | 24/6 | 5 |
| 44 | 93 | O | R | R | 24/6 | 6 |
| 45 | 94 | O | R | R | 24/6 | 7 |

At age forty-four (44), this client quit their daytime job and fully committed to their entrepreneurial desires and efforts. The twenty-four (24) of the total letter vibration encourages this client's using of their tools, abilities and assets toward returning to a simpler personal format as recommended by the *I-Ching*. The six (6) vibration talks about commitment, choice and dedication. The *personal year* six (6) vibration occurring simultaneously opened the door for this to be expressed. The (O) vibration (6) shows the physical commitment while the nine (9) emotional letter and the (9) traditional letter shows the "cleaning out the closets" vibration which simplifies this client's objectives.

The *excursion chart* is a tool that doesn't necessarily talk about prediction but gives a timed clue as to what kinds of vibration will be dominant in the client's life at any given time. The times when the total name letters add up and match the *personal year* and/or the *birth path* indicates pivotal times in the client's life experience. How these vibrations are handled determines our predictive potential, especially, in light of whether the client is open to the opportunity for growth and change that comes with the cycle or whether they are too deeply ingrained in creating and maintaining a lower mind state of security resistant to change. The client's state of mind and maturity must be carefully assessed by the reader to determine which direction will likely be chosen.

Additional information on the *excursion chart* may be found in Kevin Quinn Avery's book *The Numbers of Life: The Hidden Power of Numerology*. See recommended reading for more information.

## KABALA & ABRACADABRA METHOD

This method consists of an inverted pyramid. Its timing structure is a bit different from the *excursion chart*. It gives information in nine (9) year segments. It gives each letter of the name, beginning with the first, a nine (9) year period of the numerical cycle to manifest in. You will also notice that the life expectancy is only seventy-two (72) years. This is due to the fact that this information comes from Egyptian times when mortality was shorter.

Since the first name relates to our physical being, it's logical to assume that we may see physical manifestations as predicted. To set the chart up we will again use our friend John George Smith as an example.

Begin by setting the first nine (9) letters of the client's name in a line on the top of the page. Underneath each letter list its corresponding numerical vibration. (J=1, O=6, etc.)

Next, take each next pair of numbers, in this case starting with the one (1) and the six (6), *add* them together and reduce them if necessary to a single digit and place it in the space below the corresponding pair. This puts a seven (7) below the one (1) and the six (6). Then move on to the six (6) and the eight (8), add them together for a fourteen (14), reduce it to a five (5) and place it in the space below the six (6) and the eight (8). Follow through the row to the end in the same way. Then begin again with the line just completed. Work now with the seven (7) and the five (5). Add them together for twelve (12), reduce it to three (3) and place it below the seven (7) and the five (5).

Continue in this way completing each row until you arrive at the last single digit in the pyramid, in this case, the nine (9). We now have a full pyramid. The number at the bottom informs us of one of the most important uses of John's name vibration, namely, the streamlining quality of the nine (9) vibration. If used properly, John's name will ultimately be addressed to any capacity or occupation that utilizes a nine (9) vibration such as demolition, dentistry, medicine, psychiatry, efficiency expertise and services utilizing many hats as a qualification. If the name is *not* utilized and performed as such, John likely will *need* the services of the professions described.

We can also use the pyramid to spot specific types of energy and their timed influences determined by where they are found in the pyramid. We do this by using smaller triangles

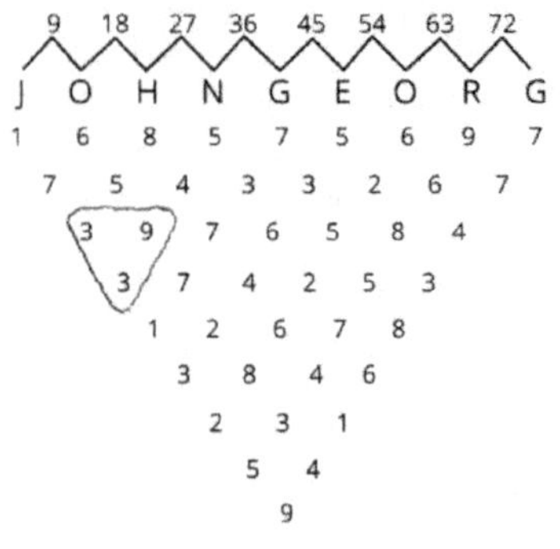

pinpointing specific types of energies and the time that may be encountered. Notice in the second diagram left that there is a thirty-nine (39) over three (3) directly under eighteen (18) years of age. The thirty-nine (39) corresponds to *obstacles* in the *I Ching*. The thirty-nine (39) reduces to a twelve (12) and then a three (3). Twelve (12) shows as *stagnation* in the *I Ching* and then to three (3) corresponding to *difficult beginnings*. If we look up the pyramid, we see that the thirty-nine (39) begins at age thirteen and a half (13.5) years of age, halfway between nine (9) and eighteen (18) and extends to approximately twenty-two and a half (22.5), halfway between eighteen (18) and twenty-seven (27) years of age. The intensity of the difficulty peaks at eighteen (18) years of age and tapers off. Generally, the *obstacles* can be either environmental circumstances or is generated internally creating the circumstances. *Obstacles* result in *stagnation* leading to *difficult beginnings*. Since it resonates in the first name, we can assume that this will involve physical issues. Either way, John will have a challenging time during most of his adolescence, whether self-generated or otherwise.

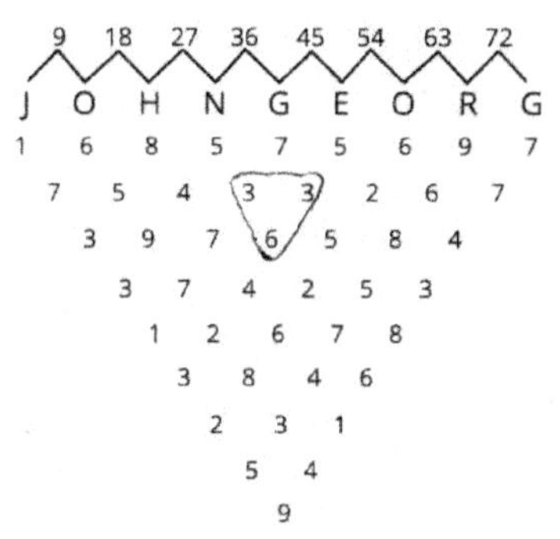


In the next triangle we see a thirty-three (33) over six (6) at age forty and a half. This is approximately at mid-life (40.5) which is normally regarded to be forty-two (42). There is something that John is *retreating* from as per the *I Ching*. You will also notice a seven (7) above it indicating an additional requirement for a detachment of some sort. This is likely to be a time where he will retreat into himself much like when we enter into a seven (7) *personal year*. This is also directly over the pyramid apex of a nine (9) which corresponds to the streamlining and personal distillation so prevalent in the nine (9) vibration. His mid-life crisis will be a function of voluntarily pulling inside and "resetting" his world views *or* have what he might be holding on to ripped away so his distractions will not prevent him from seeing himself. The choice will be his.

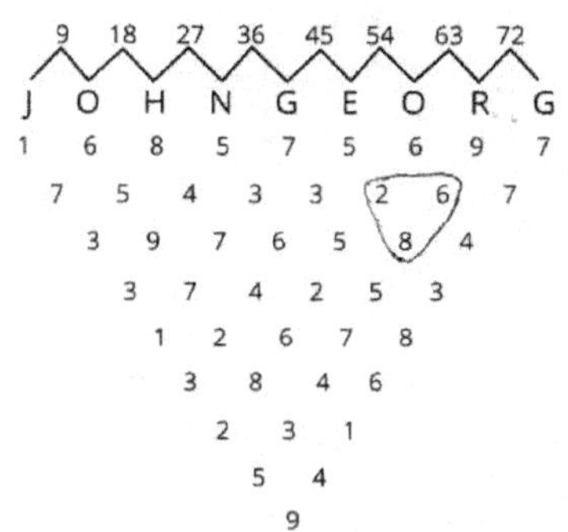


In the last triangle we see a twenty-six (26) over an eight (8) at fifty-eight and a half years of age. This is just before retirement age. At this point John is growing tremendous *potential energy* to be at his disposal as per the *I Ching*. As it reduces to the eight (8) and to be effective, it requires him to be disciplined, organized and supremely structured as per the universal forces. You will also notice another eight (8) below it further emphasizing these needs. The second eight (8) comes from a fifty-three (53) triangle below it which speaks of his *developing* as per the *I Ching*. Humility will also be required. If his ego demands that he be in authority over his environment and those around him, his acquired energy will fold into a catastrophic nose dive. The six (6) above the triangle demands commitment, proper prioritizing and clear decision making. If he is alternatively overpowered by any need to belong, he will also lose any *potential energy* gained prior to this opportunity. The choice is again his.

The *Kabala and Abracadabra Method* is an invaluable too; but only when used in conjunction with the other basic protocols. By itself, it will be misguided as there will be no foundation to base it on. More information on this method can be found in Helyn Hitchcock's book *Helping Yourself with Numerology*. See recommended reading for more information.

---

## THE NAME GRAPH

| 1 | 2 | 3 |
|---|---|---|
| 4 | 5 | 6 |
| 7 | 8 | 9 |

| AJS | BKT | CLU |
|-----|-----|-----|
| DMV | ENW | FOX |
| GPY | HQZ | IR |

The *Name Graph* also works strictly with the potential of combined letters. It's set up in the form of a tic-tac-toe board. The first board on the left shows the order positioning of the numbers. The second board on the right exchanges the letters for the corresponding letters.

Once we have determined how someone's letter totals fill the squares, we will examine which line angles are filled and which lines are missing letters. This will give us many qualities to work with in understanding what our client has to work with and what they may be lacking.

This example shows an example of what the line angles bring or not to our client.

Each plane, when *filled with all three numbers*, will offer us life qualities or circumstances through our name that will be of benefit to us. For example, when we look at the diagonal plane including three (3), five (5) and seven (7), we can see that some sense of fame or public notice will likely result from using our name in a way that aligns with universal values and protocols. The *degree* of fame or public notice will depend on many other contributing factors, but nevertheless, *some* degree will manifest. If any one of the numbers in the plane are absent, the quality of that plane will most likely be unavailable to us. With this under our belt, let's move on to a sample. For this we will return to John George Smith and his name totals.

**J o h n  G e o r g e  S m i t h**
**1 6 8 5  7 5 6 9 7 5  1 4 9 2 8**

| 2 | 1 | 0 |
|---|---|---|
| ones | Two | Threes |
| 1 | 3 | 2 |
| Four | Fives | Sixes |
| 2 | 2 | 2 |
| Sevens | Eights | Nines |

First, we need all the numbers associated with his name. Vowels, consonants or totals don't matter. We just need to know how many of each letter are present and then we then add those numbers corresponding to each of the signified letters into each of their appropriate squares.

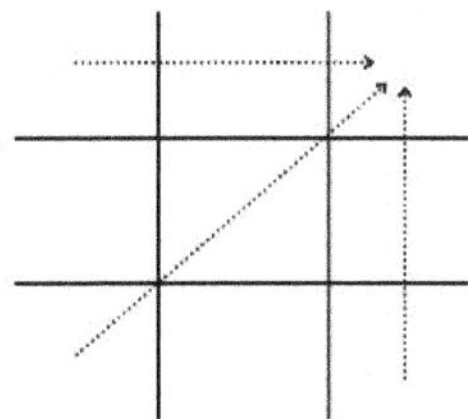

We can immediately see that there is an absence of C's, L's or U's in his name. That means that he not only has no threes (3's) in his name but that one of his numerological placements will remain is empty. That contributes toward leaving three planes of action incomplete: from the bottom right up (3-6-9), from the top left toward the right (1- 2-3) and from the bottom left diagonally up to the top right (3-5-7). This doesn't mean that he hasn't any of the qualities assigned to those planes but that he will have to work harder at developing his ability for *expansiveness* (3) in order to make those planes perform for him. So, in order to make his *career* perform well it will require extra *dedication* (plane 1-2-3). In order to accomplish *public notice* or *fame*, he will have to actively promote

himself (plane 3-5-7). And in order to develop *higher thinking* or a comprehension of the *abstract* he will have to study harder than most (plane 3-6-9).

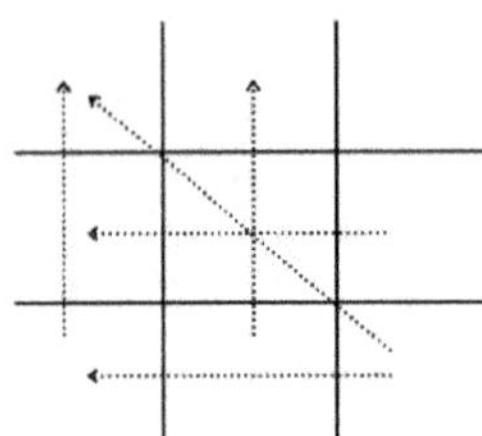

Now let's take a look at what he *has* going for him. There are five planes where he

planes where he has qualities and circumstances that will come a bit more easily. Plane (1-4-7) gives him the ability to muster superior energy for *labor* and *work*. With this he has additional force, power and influence through plane (7-8-9). These forces along with plane (1-5-9) essentially ensures that *material success* will be relatively smooth and easy. This will compound with plane (4-5-6) of *home, arts* and *beauty*. And finally, plane (2-5-8) brings feeling, *emotion*, a sense of something more than just the fruits of the physical world like the *soul* and a blossoming growth of recognizing universal cause and effect through *karma*. Remembering his seven (7) *birth path*, we can also understand how plane (1-4-7) of *labor* and *work* and plane (7-8-9) of *force, power* and *influence* might have particular significance for him. We can also understand how the withdrawing and detachment brought through that seven (7) *birth path* might draw his attention to plane (3-5-7) of *fame* and *public notice* making it a "sore spot" for his desires and efforts (notice the absence of the three (3)).

In and of themselves, completed or empty planes neither provide nor deprive our client from manifesting their influences. Completed, they simply provide an easier and smoother path toward their facilitation. Our client's accumulated attitudes and choice of actions will determine whether these qualities and circumstances will ever actually manifest. Let's look a little more closely at each plane of influence and see what driving forces exist behind them.

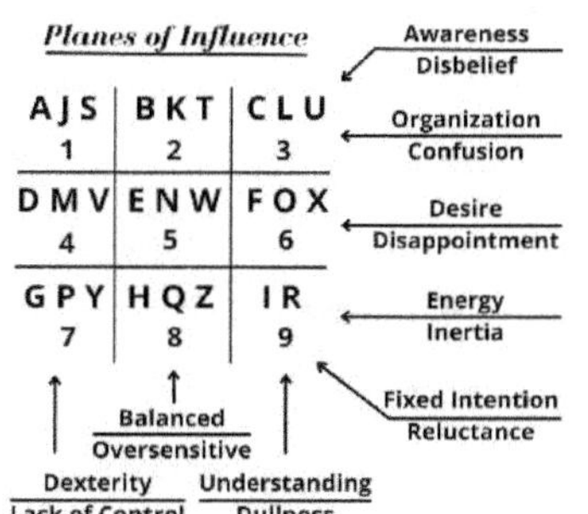


In order that these planes may manifest there is a headspace or mindset that orchestrates what will happen. This headspace is a function of the maturity of the individual. If we are open to change and possibility, the energy flows freely and manifests easily. If we are locked into our own personal mindset based on what we believe the world is presenting to us, we can easily misinterpret our situations and end up blocking the very thing we are striving for. Let's take a look at each of the planes to understand the interaction between our attitudes and what is manifested.

**Plane (1-2-3)** – *Dedication & Career* – Having a career that is strong is usually a function or our attentiveness, awareness and dedications. It requires focus and a strong sense of what is needed along with how it must be organized. Organization usually sets the foundation for the result of our efforts that follow. It's a process of conscious building. It takes patience and a willingness to allow the world to respond to what we have set in motions. If we are confused or disorganized, whatever we have intended will likely not manifest due to the lack of cohesiveness or consistency normally inherent in being organized and dedicated in our efforts.

**Plane (4-5-6)** – *Home, Arts & Beauty* – Beauty is in the eye of the beholder. If we are wrapped up in only what we personally need or want, that sense of beauty will be narrow and selfishly limiting based on what preserves the security of our ego. But if we are able to perceive the unity of our presence in the universe and feel humility in reference to it, we can sense the awe and peace of its magnificence. This becomes an acceptance of the world as it is. Our greatest desire is to be accepted and accept ourselves as we are. If we are and do, our world becomes peaceful and beautiful, and this becomes reflected in our home and environment. If that desire is not achieved, disappointment ensues and nothing that we have will be appreciated.

**Plane (7-8-9)** – *Force, power & Influence* – These qualities represent a momentum in our preferred direction. Their initiation comes from qualities such as inspiration, encouragement, ambition and desire for things that spur a person into action. It is a function of an individual's willingness to initiate action and *energy* and continue along a path to its completion. When an individual only allows *inertia* to dictate, no amount of hoping or wishing will change what the universe has already been sending to us. *Force, power & influence* require personal initiative and a self-generated push if we are to expect the universe to be redirected toward our benefit.

**Plane (1-4-7)** – *Labor & Work* - When we maintain a disciplined and conscious effort in any direction, by virtue of natural law, these energies must produce a manifestation. Whether that manifestation is one of resistance or alliance, a response from the universe is inevitable. This discipline is a function of *self-control* and *focused dexterity* whether physically, emotionally, or mentally. The consistent energy builds on itself until the universe can no longer ignore the force and yields itself toward our chosen direction. If our desires and effort are inconsistent and intermittent, our energy dissipates long before the force of its focus can manifest a response from the universe. Our *work* and *labor* are then in vain.

**Plane (2-5-8)** - *Emotion, Soul & Karma* – To have and then acknowledge our feelings is a function of our awareness. That awareness leads us toward being aware of a world or existence beyond the recognition of our personal space. When we become aware of the world beyond us, we are more likely to be able to perceive and understand the karmic returns that the world presents to us as a result of our participation in it. When we can see the developing patterns, we become aware enough to recognize how we create what the world presents to us giving us the opportunity to adjust those patterns and release any karmic obligations we might have engendered. When we are *insensitive* or *oversensitive* as a result of being out of balance and only in a reactive state, we miss the meaning behind what the universe presents us with and are unable to address our karma due to that lack of awareness. This obscures any recognition of our soul or spirit identity affirming that we are "of the world" rather than simply "in it" and taking a conscious and active role in its shaping.

**Plane (3-6-9)** - *Higher Thinking & Abstract* – To see beyond ourselves as an active part in shaping the world we perceive is a gift. This requires an *understanding* of the interaction between the influences we present to the world and the responses we receive from it as a consequence. This involves recognizing the world beyond our own space and our participation in it. This enables us to see the patterns that we alone have set in motion. As we view the patterns, we can perceive the abstract qualities of their organization and make analogies to countless other aspects of life that bear the same patterning. If we cannot detach ourselves and move beyond our own limited patterns of thinking, we will exist solely in a mindset beset by the ignorance and *dullness* symptomatic of only the material world.

**Plane (1-5-9)** – *Material Success* – *Material success* is a manifestation of living life and working within the realms of our own values and natural inclinations. These natural inclinations fix our *intentions* and provide a consistency in the application of our energy. They can be powered by either altruism or obsessiveness. Altruism usually considers others in our endeavors. Obsessiveness usually negates them. What we consider success depends on our perspective of what we believe life is supposed to offer us and whom we are ultimately responsible to and for. It is different for every person since every person's experience and values are different. Some people simply want peace, others want a rich and extravagant life. What enables us to arrive at that point is a function of our *intentions.* If we are *reluctant* to focus our intentions or exert the effort, we usually find ourselves defined by failure, if not by our own definition, by those whom we allow to judge us.

**Plane (3-5-7)** – *Fame & Public Notice* – When people find what we do influences them to any extent, good or bad, we gain *public notice.* Advertising will also gain *public notice,* either as something completely different from what people expect or through finding that what is advertised might provide advantage toward something that they desire. *Fame* is *public notice* through an extreme as compared to daily occurrences and creates notice in a broader number of people. *Fame* is usually sought to assuage feelings of personal inferiority or simply a desire for some kind of personal recognition. Whether it comes through our desires initiated through intentional actions or as a result of actions we've taken *without* an ulterior motive, it is a function of creating awareness in others of who or what we are based on what we have done or broadcasted. If our *awareness* is focused on what others think of us, *fame* or *public notice* usually backfires through our tendency to over-play it. *Disbelief,* ours and that of others, then takes precedence. Immature and insecure people usually focus more on themselves and what other people think of them than any other issue. If we are not overly self-conscious and our *awareness* is focused on a project or action that benefits both us and others, *fame* or *public notice* usually comes naturally and easily.

More information on this method can be found in *A Handbook for Numerologists* by William Alan Schneider and Aline R. Gray.

# IN SUMMARY

I have covered a number of perspectives that are not examined in other numerology books. I have *not* covered many of the technical variations that other books cover simply because another rehashing of the same material will benefit very few beyond what has been already delineated. I have endeavored to present a fresh perspective that deals more with the energetic currents present in our own attempts to see things in more of an intangible perspective and geared toward our spiritual growth and understanding rather than the usual and more common place predictive expectations.

# *References & Helpful Reading* Material


Avery, Kevin Quinn, (1974). *The Numbers of Life: The Hidden Power in Numerology*. Doubleday & Company, Inc., Garden City, New York. ISBN# 0-385-12629-8.

Blakney, Raymond Bernard, (1955). *The Way of Life Lao Tzu*: Tao Te Ching A New Translation. The New American Library, Inc., New York, New York. Library of Congress Card No. 55-7401.

Heline, Corinne, (1981). *The Sacred Science of Numbers*. DeVorss & Company Publisher, Marina del Rey, California. ISBN# 0-87516-442-0.

Hitchcock, Helyn, (1972). *Helping Yourself with Numerology*. Parker Publishing Company, Inc., West Nyack, New York. ISBN# 978-0133867565.

Line, Julia, (1985). *The Numerology Workbook: Understanding and Using the Power of Numbers*. The Aquarian Press, Northamptonshire, England. ISBN# 0-85030-425-3.

Millman, Dan, (1993). *The Life You Were Born to Live*. MJF Books, New York, New York. ISBN# 1-56731-398-1.

Schneider, William Alan & Gray, Alien R., (1980). *A Handbook for Numerologists*. Schneider Corporation, Ft. Wayne, Ind. WASARG: 0-11-1-628:1080/648.

Wing, R.L., (1979). *The I Ching Workbook*. Doubleday & Company, Inc., Garden City, New York. ISBN# 0-385-12838-X.

# APPENDIX

# 64 HEXAGRAMS of the I CHING

| | | | |
|---|---|---|---|
| 1 The Creative | 17 Following | 33 Retreat | 49 Revolution |
| 2 Natural Response | 18 Decay / Repair | 34 Great Power | 50 Cosmic Order |
| 3 Difficult Beginnings | 19 Approach | 35 Progress | 51 Shocking |
| 4 Inexperience | 20 Contemplate | 36 Eclipse | 52 Meditation |
| 5 Patience | 21 Reform | 37 Family | 53 Developing |
| 6 Conflict | 22 Grace | 38 Opposition | 54 Subordinate |
| 7 The Army | 23 Splitting Apart | 39 Obstacles | 55 Zenith |
| 8 Unity | 24 Returning | 40 Liberation | 56 Traveling |
| 9 Restrained | 25 Innocence | 41 Decline | 57 Gentle Penetration |
| 10 Conduct | 26 Potential Energy | 42 Benefit | 58 Encouraging |
| 11 Peace | 27 Nourishing | 43 Resolution | 59 Dispersion |
| 12 Stagnation | 28 Critical Mass | 44 Dynamic Action | 60 Limitations |
| 13 Brotherhood | 29 The Abyss | 45 Assembling | 61 Insight |
| 14 Sovereignty | 30 Synergy | 46 Advancement | 62 Conscientiousness |
| 15 Moderation | 31 Attraction | 47 Adversity | 63 After the End |
| 16 Harmonize | 32 Enduring | 48 The Well | 64 Before the End |

# THE EXCURSION CHART

| Age | YR | F | M | L | T | PY |
|---|---|---|---|---|---|---|
| 0 | | | | | | |
| 1 | | | | | | |
| 2 | | | | | | |
| 3 | | | | | | |
| 4 | | | | | | |
| 5 | | | | | | |
| 6 | | | | | | |
| 7 | | | | | | |
| 8 | | | | | | |
| 9 | | | | | | |
| 10 | | | | | | |
| 11 | | | | | | |
| 12 | | | | | | |
| 13 | | | | | | |
| 14 | | | | | | |
| 15 | | | | | | |
| 16 | | | | | | |
| 17 | | | | | | |
| 18 | | | | | | |
| 19 | | | | | | |
| 20 | | | | | | |
| 21 | | | | | | |
| 22 | | | | | | |
| 23 | | | | | | |
| 24 | | | | | | |
| 25 | | | | | | |
| 26 | | | | | | |
| 27 | | | | | | |
| 28 | | | | | | |

| Age | YR | F | M | L | T | PY |
|---|---|---|---|---|---|---|
| 29 | | | | | | |
| 30 | | | | | | |
| 31 | | | | | | |
| 32 | | | | | | |
| 33 | | | | | | |
| 34 | | | | | | |
| 35 | | | | | | |
| 36 | | | | | | |
| 37 | | | | | | |
| 38 | | | | | | |
| 39 | | | | | | |
| 40 | | | | | | |
| 41 | | | | | | |
| 42 | | | | | | |
| 43 | | | | | | |
| 44 | | | | | | |
| 45 | | | | | | |
| 46 | | | | | | |
| 47 | | | | | | |
| 48 | | | | | | |
| 49 | | | | | | |
| 50 | | | | | | |
| 51 | | | | | | |
| 52 | | | | | | |
| 53 | | | | | | |
| 54 | | | | | | |
| 55 | | | | | | |
| 56 | | | | | | |

| Age | YR | F | M | L | T | PY |
|---|---|---|---|---|---|---|
| 57 | | | | | | |
| 58 | | | | | | |
| 59 | | | | | | |
| 60 | | | | | | |
| 61 | | | | | | |
| 62 | | | | | | |
| 63 | | | | | | |
| 64 | | | | | | |
| 65 | | | | | | |
| 66 | | | | | | |
| 67 | | | | | | |
| 68 | | | | | | |
| 69 | | | | | | |
| 70 | | | | | | |
| 71 | | | | | | |
| 72 | | | | | | |
| 73 | | | | | | |
| 74 | | | | | | |
| 75 | | | | | | |
| 76 | | | | | | |
| 77 | | | | | | |
| 78 | | | | | | |
| 79 | | | | | | |
| 80 | | | | | | |
| 81 | | | | | | |
| 82 | | | | | | |
| 83 | | | | | | |
| 84 | | | | | | |

# ABRACADABRA or
# PYRAMID METHOD

| Birth | 4.5 | 9 | 13.5 | 18 | 22.5 | 27 | 31.5 | 36 | 40.5 | 45 | 49.5 | 54 | 58.5 | 63 | 67.5 | 72 |
|---|---|---|---|---|---|---|---|---|---|---|---|---|---|---|---|---|

# THE NAME GRAPH

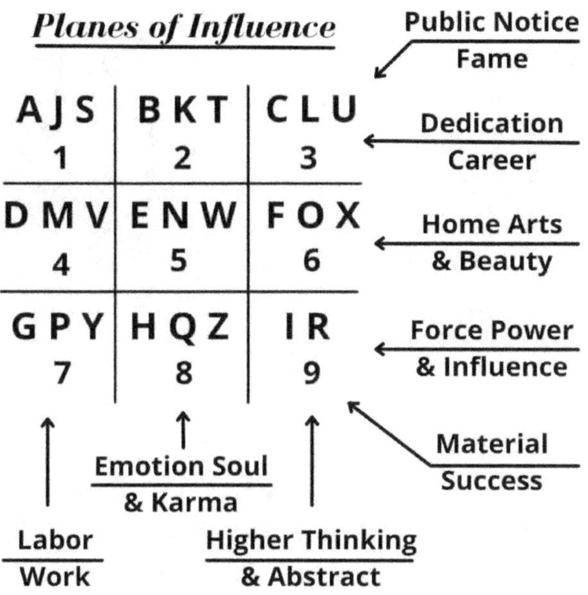


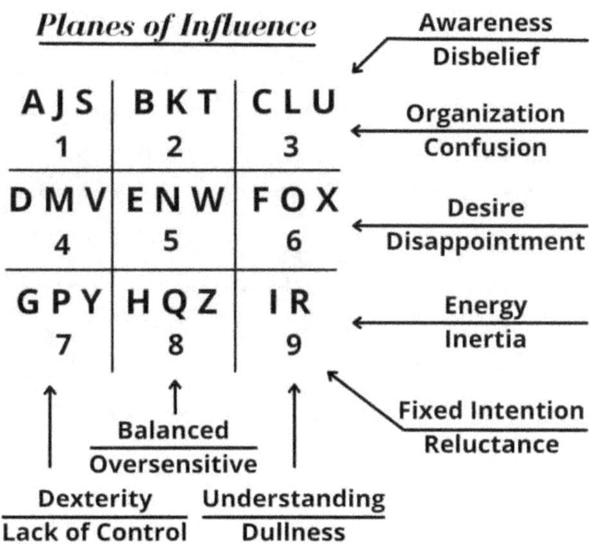

# ABOUT THE AUTHOR

John Lawrence Maerz is an author, instructor and professional speaker with specializations in metaphysics and psychology. His extensive background in metaphysical disciplines includes astrology, tarot, numerology, I-Ching, energy work, martial arts, psychic development and mediumship.

John has worked as a counselor and case manager with teen substance abuse, in child protection services and is a seasoned personal coach and adviser with diverse experience in the field of human potential. He incorporates and integrates personality influences, shadow work, nutritional needs, creative expression and personal desires while uncovering his client's innate abilities and potential.

John co-owned and successfully ran Starchild, a metaphysical bookstore in Port Charlotte, Florida, from 1995-2005. He also co-owned and ran the Astrological Institute of Integrated Studies begun in Bayshore New York, a school teaching a multitude of metaphysical subjects from 1983-1989 and in Florida from 1989-2005. He is dedicated to raising awareness and sharing his own unique perspective and understanding about life's journey and its meaning. He recognizes and emphasizes the importance of having balance and accountability. He challenges his students and clients to keep fulfilling their spiritual potential through their own individual experiences.

Over the years, John has produced a series of books, workshops, lectures and seminars presenting different metaphysical topics in print and on MP3. These materials are available on JohnMaerz.com. He is also a voracious writer and has written more than 85 articles on many thought-provoking subjects which are also available on his site. He has also published fifteen books on metaphysics and psychology.

You can contact John at **(941) 286-1562**
or at **JM@JohnMaerz.com**